ROUTLEDGE LIBRARY EDITIONS: THE ENGLISH LANGUAGE

Volume 18

PATTERN IN ENGLISH

PATTERN IN ENGLISH
A Fresh Approach to Grammar

W. H. MITTINS

LONDON AND NEW YORK

First published in 1950

This edition first published in 2015
by Routledge
2 Park Square, Milton Park, Abingdon, Oxon OX14 4RN

and by Routledge
711 Third Avenue, New York, NY 10017

Routledge is an imprint of the Taylor & Francis Group, an informa business

© 1950 W. H. Mittins

All rights reserved. No part of this book may be reprinted or reproduced or utilised in any form or by any electronic, mechanical, or other means, now known or hereafter invented, including photocopying and recording, or in any information storage or retrieval system, without permission in writing from the publishers.

Trademark notice: Product or corporate names may be trademarks or registered trademarks, and are used only for identification and explanation without intent to infringe.

British Library Cataloguing in Publication Data
A catalogue record for this book is available from the British Library

ISBN: 978-1-138-92111-5 (Set)
ISBN: 978-1-315-68654-7 (Set) (ebk)
ISBN: 978-1-138-91711-8 (Volume 18) (hbk)
ISBN: 978-1-315-68923-4 (Volume 18) (ebk)

Publisher's Note
The publisher has gone to great lengths to ensure the quality of this reprint but points out that some imperfections in the original copies may be apparent.

Disclaimer
The publisher has made every effort to trace copyright holders and would welcome correspondence from those they have been unable to trace.

PATTERN IN ENGLISH

A FRESH APPROACH TO GRAMMAR

BY

W. H. MITTINS
B.A.

LONDON
GEORGE ALLEN & UNWIN LTD

FIRST PUBLISHED IN 1950

This book is copyright under the Berne Convention. No portion may be reproduced by any process without written permission. Inquiries should be addressed to the publishers

PRINTED IN GREAT BRITAIN
in 11 on 12 pt. Baskerville type
AT THE UNIVERSITY PRESS
ABERDEEN

FOREWORD

This book includes what seems to me the minimum of English grammar relevant to efficient communication in language. The scope was determined by collecting from children's writings examples of common faults and weaknesses susceptible of treatment in grammatical terms. Certain concepts emerged as fundamental—predication, word-order, proximity, equivalents, variety and repetition. Other notions helped towards the clear exposition of these fundamentals—parts of speech, phrases, clauses, link-words. Some time-honoured ideas—notably the classification of the parts of speech into categories: concrete and abstract nouns, demonstrative and possessive adjectives, and so on—seemed unnecessary.

Apart from a few matters relegated to appendices, this material is organised on a simple plan which, while easy for reference, provides a progressive course, leading from the structure of the simple sentence to problems of literary style.

The Simple Sentence is shown to be an assembly, according to one of a well-defined range of patterns, of various items. These items are certain Parts of Speech or their equivalents. Equivalents include other Parts of Speech (acting, as it were, out of character), Phrases, and Clauses.

The assembling of the items involves the principle of Proximity and the use of Conjunctions and other link-words. The notions of Co-ordination and Subordination and the earlier reference to Clauses as Equivalents lead to an examination of Multiple Sentences, with their Main and Subordinate Clauses.

Finally, the various word-clusters (Phrases and Clauses) are seen at work in passages from competent authors. The stylistic principles of emphasis, variety and repetition are associated with the distribution of phrases and clauses in consecutive prose.

To keep the central sequence of the argument clear, some important considerations are denied separate treatment. There are not, for instance, separate chapters on the Parts of Speech. A few minor points—Person and Number, for instance—are not introduced in the text at all, but in the exercises.

There are, I suppose, never enough exercises in a text-book. The teacher should have no difficulty, however, in expanding those given here. It is to be hoped, moreover, that they will be linked with an examination both of the pupils' own writing and of the literature being studied.

The practical core of the exercises is analysis. Some teachers deplore the schematic approach. Others who like schemes have their own favourite systems. The stencil method outlined in Chapter XXXI is, I believe, original and may appeal to those who, like myself, find that the more popular systems fail effectively to expose the bare bones of a sentence. Not wishing, nevertheless, to dogmatise in so controversial a matter, I have confined the stencil suggestion to an appendix, to which unobtrusive references are made in the course of the text.

FOREWORD

Opinions vary considerably as to the age at which grammar should be taught. I have aimed primarily at the middle and upper forms of grammar schools. But, suitably diluted, the book should be usable both by junior grammar school forms and by other secondary pupils. A fair amount of guidance from teachers is assumed, but older students—in evening classes, for instance—should be able to manage unaided.

W. H. M.

ACKNOWLEDGEMENTS

Acknowledgement is due to the following for permission to use copyright material :—

Mr. John Farquharson, for extract from Thomas Burke's *Old Joe*.

Messrs. Cassell & Co., Ltd., and the author, for extracts from Winston Churchill's *War Memoirs*, Volume 2.

Messrs. Longmans, Green & Co., Ltd., and the author, for extract from Professor G. M. Trevelyan's *English Social History*.

Mr. A. D. Peters and the author, for extract from Hilaire Belloc's *First and Last*.

Messrs. Cassell & Co., Ltd., for extract from G. K. Chesterton's *Three Tools of Death*.

Messrs. J. M. Dent & Sons, Ltd., for extract from Joseph Conrad's *Youth*.

Dr. John Masefield, O.M., and the Society of Authors, for extract from *A Tarpaulin Muster*.

Messrs. Longmans, Green & Co., Ltd., for extract from Lieut.-Colonel Henderson's *Stonewall Jackson*.

I must also thank Miss Nancy Martin, Lecturer on the Teaching of English at London University Institute of Education, for a number of most helpful criticisms and suggestions.

CONTENTS

FOREWORD	*page*	5
ACKNOWLEDGEMENTS		8

PART I—SIMPLE SENTENCES

Chapter
I.	Sentence and Predication	11
II.	Two-Item Basis: Subject and Verb	15
III.	Three-Item Basis: Direct Object	26
IV.	Three-Item Basis: Subject-Complement	31
V.	Four-Item Basis: Indirect Object	36
VI.	Four-Item Basis: Object-Complement	41
VII.	Word-Order: Commands, Questions, Exclamations	45
VIII.	Case	50

PART II—EQUIVALENTS

IX.	Word, Phrase and Clause	53
X.	Verb-Equivalents	58
XI.	Noun-Equivalents	62
XII.	Adjective-Equivalents	69
XIII.	Adverb-Equivalents	79
XIV.	Revision	85

PART III—ASSEMBLING THE ITEMS

XV.	Proximity	91
XVI.	Link-Words	95

PART IV—MULTIPLE SENTENCES

Chapter		
XVII.	Compound Sentences *page*	100
XVIII.	Complex Sentences: Adjective Clauses	104
XIX.	Complex Sentences: Adverb Clauses	110
XX.	Complex Sentences: Noun Clauses	115
XXI.	Compound-Complex Sentences	119
XXII.	Revision	121

PART V—PARAGRAPH PATTERNS

XXIII.	Introduction: Variety *v.* Repetition	124
XXIV.	Number of Word-Clusters	126
XXV.	Kind of Word-Clusters	132
XXVI.	Order of Word-Clusters	139

PART VI—APPENDICES

XXVII.	Appendix A: Prepositions, Adverbs and Conjunctions	145
XXVIII.	Appendix B: Adverbs and Adjectives	148
XXIX.	Appendix C: Prepositions	150
XXX.	Appendix D: Tense	152
XXXI.	Appendix E: Stencil Analysis	159
	Index	161

PART ONE
SIMPLE SENTENCES

CHAPTER I
SENTENCE AND PREDICATION

Read this passage aloud:—

As I reached the inn door I heard voices raised in angry argument. I hesitated a moment. Then I gently pushed the door open and peered in. The room was crowded. A tall strong man, with a tarry pigtail hanging over his shoulders. The landlord was crouching in the corner.

Correct the statement that sounds wrong, by adding to it.

EXERCISE

Similarly, make sentences of the following:—

(i) The house on top of the hill near Dunscombe . . .
(ii) The mudguards of the dilapidated old bicycle . . .
(iii) Novels like the Biggles series by Capt. W. E. Johns . . .
(iv) Tigers, leopards and cheetahs . . .
(v) The railings round the football ground . . .

(vi) Mr. Winston Churchill . . .
(vii) Coal-miners, whose work is very hard and unpleasant, . . .
(viii) Feeling weary after his long day in the hot sun, John . . .
(ix) One of the drawbacks of fishing as a pastime . . .
(x) The man to whom Captain Flint gave his sea-chest when he was dying at Savannah . . .

*　　*　　*

You have in the above exercise made sentences by saying something about the things mentioned. The thing mentioned is called the SUBJECT; the statement about it is the PREDICATE. The two together—Subject plus Predicate—may be called a PREDICATION.

Every sentence should contain at least one Predication.

Usually the Subject comes first, but sometimes this order is reversed :—

(a) Round the corner came *an errand boy on a bicycle.*

Sometimes the Subject is sandwiched in the middle of the Predicate :—

(b) The next day *the two boys* returned to the beach.

Sometimes the Predicate is sandwiched between parts of the Subject :—

(c) The Captain *leapt to his feet,* indignant at the interruption.

Notice that: in (b) 'the next day' belongs with 'returned';
in (c) 'indignant at the interruption' belongs with 'captain'

EXERCISES

A. Divide the following sentences into Subjects and Predicates :—

   (i) Playing with fire is a dangerous occupation.
   (ii) The horse suddenly bolted down the street.
   (iii) At the cross-roads it narrowly missed a tram.
   (iv) Underneath the heap of rubble was an iron-bound chest full of documents.
   (v) The negro shrank into the corner, terrified by the approaching flames.
   (vi) Mr. Johnson always sat in the armchair under the window.
   (vii) Every morning John and Mary practised their duet.
   (viii) Mr. and Mrs. Smith and their family sat fascinated by the performance.
   (ix) At the end of the programme came a trumpet solo.
   (x) Near the end of the fight the favourite collapsed.

B. Punctuate the following passage so that each Predication forms one sentence :—

The performance was timed to begin at seven o'clock parents and friends took their seats well before the actors were ready and in a state of high excitement behind the curtain the stage hands were checking the properties in the wings the electrician was standing by to turn out the house lights at a signal from the stage-manager he pressed a switch in the hall the audience stopped talking amid a hush of expectancy the curtain rose.

C. Express as short Predications the meaning of the following:—

No Litter.
Free Air.
Adults Only.
No Circulars.
Low Bridge Ahead.
Out of Bounds.
All Change!
Unsafe for Bathers.
One Way Only.

No Admittance except on Business.

D. Make five sentences by linking each Subject with its Predicate, dovetailing them where necessary:—

SUBJECTS	PREDICATES
the three boys	are in the wood-wind section of the orchestra
the chairman . . . irritated by the interruption	at ten o'clock exactly . . .
feeling cold, he	rode into the lists at the bottom of the garden . . . found an old chest
flutes, oboes and clarinets	glared round
the two knights . . . armed to the teeth	fetched some more coal

CHAPTER II

TWO-ITEM BASIS: SUBJECT AND VERB

A normal sentence contains at least one Predication. A Predication consists of Subject plus Predicate. Therefore the shortest possible sentence should contain two words, of the pattern:—

SUBJECT	PREDICATE
Wasps	sting
She	fainted

How, then, can we explain one-word sentences such as:—

Stop!
Listen!

These words resemble Predicates rather than Subjects. The missing Subject, as in all commands and instructions, is 'you':—

SUBJECT	PREDICATE
(You)	stop!

In sentences like 'Yes' and 'No' the whole Predication is implied without being stated. In:—

'Can you hear me?'
'No.'

—'No' stands for:—

SUBJECT	PREDICATE
I	cannot

The technical name for leaving out words in this way is Ellipsis. For the purpose of grammar the implied words must be treated as if openly stated. With this proviso, we may work on the assumption that the shortest sentence contains two words.

EXERCISE

Complete or supply the implied Predication (not necessarily in two words) in:—

(i) Look!
(ii) Coming?
(iii) Stand up straight!
(iv) ('I have mended your bicycle tyre.') 'Good.'
(v) ('Would you care to buy a flag?') 'No.'

* * *

What kinds of words can be used as Subjects and Predicates? Make a list of two-word sentences like these:—

SUBJECT	PREDICATE
Time	flies
Nobody	arrived
He	resigned
Fishermen	exaggerate
We	exist

The Subject is either (a) a NOUN—it names what the sentence is about; or (b) a PRONOUN—it stands for a Noun previously mentioned or understood.

The Predicate is a VERB—it indicates what the Subject 'does' or 'is'.

A two-item Predication may be formulated as:—

SUBJECT plus PREDICATE
Who? What?   does/is
Noun/Pronoun   Verb

A Sentence which contains only one Predication is called a SIMPLE SENTENCE. Most Simple Sentences naturally contain more than two words, but the two-item basis of Subject plus Verb can always be found:—

The one-eyed *man* sitting in the corner *coughed* loudly.

EXERCISE

Identify the two-item basis in the following:—

(i) All through the night the wind howled round the house.
(ii) Nevertheless Jack slept soundly.
(iii) The next morning he awoke refreshed.
(iv) Dressing quickly he went downstairs and out into the garden.
(v) Up the path came two fierce-looking mastiffs, barking and growling ominously.
(vi) Our hero, mistrusting them, promptly withdrew into the house.
(vii) Just inside the French windows stood an old writing-desk.
(viii) Jack, by now thoroughly mystified, hesitated for a moment.
(ix) He stood staring at the desk.

(x) Then, breathing hard, the young boy stepped forward.

* * *

Examine these sentences:—

(a) My *brother works* in Manchester.
(b) He is working in a leather factory.
(c) He has worked for some time in Manchester.
(d) He used to work ten hours a day.
(e) He will not be working on Christmas Day.

In (b) to (e) the basic Subject corresponding to 'brother' in (a) is obviously 'he'. But what corresponds to the basic Verb 'works'? 'Working', 'worked', etc., are not enough. The notion of 'doing' is contained in the word-groups:—

(b) is working
(c) has worked
(d) used to work
(e) will not be working

We shall treat word-groups like these—including combinations with 'may', 'might', 'ought', 'should', and so on—as if they were single words, even when the group is split (e.g. He *ought* in fact *to have been working*). That is why we talk of *two-item*, rather than *two-word*, Predications.

EXERCISES

A. Find the two-item basis in:—

(i) Most of the children were playing in the fields.

SUBJECT AND VERB

(ii) Isabel ought to have been helping in the house.
(iii) Her father would not be returning until nightfall.
(iv) He had on a few occasions stayed at Capel overnight.
(v) But he could not in the circumstances be expected to do so this time.
(vi) Mother is lying in bed sick.
(vii) The doctor will have left by now.
(viii) He does not often come here.
(ix) He must have left by the back door.
(x) I shall, all being well, go to church next Sunday.

B. The two basic items—Noun/Pronoun and Verb—must agree in number; i.e. both Singular or both Plural. Choose the correct alternative in each of the following:—

(i) The House of Lords *are/is* less powerful than the House of Commons.
(ii) Immediately the house and shop *was/were* ablaze.
(iii) A certain shepherd, with his flock of sheep, *are/is* on an island.
(iv) Each of them *was/were* tried by the Inquisition.
(v) The reason why the sails are hoisted *is/are* that the boat is expected to leave soon.
(vi) A vast area of the Alps *are/is* in Switzerland.
(vii) Neither Tom nor Dick *was/were* at the rehearsal last night.
(viii) One or the other of us *are/is* bound to be caught.

(ix) The security of a safe job and a comfortable home *become/becomes* more attractive as the years pass.

(x) Physics *seem/seems* to be his strongest subject.

* * *

The Verb in the basis of a Sentence may, we have seen, contain one or more words. It may be of the patterns:—

    (*a*) (I) hope, hoped
or (*b*) (I) am hoping, may hope, have hoped, etc.
or (*c*) (I) shall be hoping, might have hoped, ought to hope, etc.
or (*d*) (I) shall have been hoping, ought to have hoped, etc.

From these examples it is clear that, whereas 'hope' and 'hoped' may or may not be complete Verbs, 'hoping' is never complete. It is not possible to make a Predication by putting a Subject and nothing else in front of it. In other words, 'hoping' is not a FINITE VERB. It is a Participle and, to become Finite, needs the addition of another Verb—an AUXILIARY VERB—

$$\text{AUXILIARY} + \frac{\text{PRESENT}}{\text{PARTICIPLE}} = \text{FINITE VERB}$$

    am   +   hoping   = am hoping

The form in -ing is the PRESENT PARTICIPLE. It is easily recognised as non-Finite, because with a Subject but without an Auxiliary Verb it can never make a Predication.

But the PAST PARTICIPLE is not so easy to recognise, because it is commonly spelt the same as the Finite Past Tense.

(a)		(b)	
PAST TENSE	PAST PARTICIPLE	PAST TENSE	PAST PARTICIPLE
swam	swum	walked	walked
fell	fallen	crept	crept
swelled	swollen	told	told
burned	burnt	bound	bound

The Past Participles under (*a*) are obviously not Finite, since it would never be possible to make a Predication by adding merely a Subject. But those under (*b*) must be seen in the sentences to which they belong:—

Compare: He *bound* his enemy hand and foot.
with: *Bound* hand and foot, he was quite helpless.

In the latter sentence the need for an Auxiliary Verb as well as a Subject (e.g. he *had been* bound) indicates that this 'bound' is not Finite:—

$$\text{AUXILIARY} + \frac{\text{PAST}}{\text{PARTICIPLE}} = \text{FINITE VERB}$$

had been   +   bound   = had been bound

There remains the Verb-Form with 'to': *to* hope, *to* have hoped, etc. This is the INFINITIVE.

When 'to' is actually stated the Verb is clearly not Finite. Sometimes, however, the 'to' is dropped:—

Nobody saw him *go*.
Let us *begin*.

Summing up: The Verb in the basis of a sentence must be a Finite Verb and not a non-Finite Verb (Participle or Infinitive).

EXERCISES

A. Pick out the non-Finite Verbs in the following and classify them as Present/Past Participles or Infinitives:—

Delighted to find himself remembered in the home town which he had not seen during his seven years' absence, Captain Barnes strode briskly down the street, swinging his cane and whistling cheerfully. Arrived at No. 10, he knocked loudly on the door and stepped back to enjoy the amazement he expected to cause. But, to his dismay, as he stood there smiling confidently, the door was opened only a few inches and a harsh voice barked at him: 'Go away! I've got no money to waste on hawkers!'

B. Correct the following sentences by making the Verbs Finite:—

(i) The Prince knowing the officers were going to kill him.
(ii) The climbers, exhausted by their struggle against the blizzard and their vain attempts to reach the summit.
(iii) After long discussion and argument a treaty signed by the opposing commanders-in-chief.
(iv) (As you go along the road to Deal you pass many old windmills.) The one near Martin Mill Station being particularly old.

(v) (In big city libraries there are different departments.) The book-binding department being one of them.

C. Write pairs of sentences in which the following words are used firstly as Finite Verbs, secondly as Past Participles:—

>washed, brought, filled, held, stopped, cut, caught, arranged, found, packed.

* * *

Extracting the two-item basis from:

>Strong *winds swept* across the plain

—we are left with 'strong' and 'across the plain'. What do these two items do in the sentence?

The word 'strong' tells us what sort of winds they were; the word-group 'across the plain' tells us where they swept. Each adds something to one of the basic items. In grammatical language it extends (or limits or qualifies or modifies) the Noun/Pronoun or Verb.

A word or word-group which extends a Noun or Pronoun, answering questions such as which?, what sort of?, or how many? about it, is ADJECTIVAL.

The extension of a Verb, telling us where, when, why, how, etc., the action took place, is ADVERBIAL.

Our sentence can therefore be represented:—

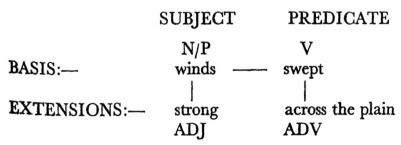

Extensions are variable in number. There may be none at all. On the other hand, there may be several attached to a single item:—

For three nights the escaped convict, hungry and exhausted, hid in a barn.

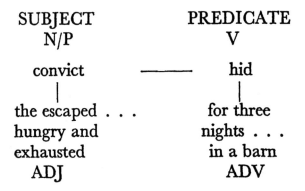

(See Chapter XXXI. If the stencil device is to be used, now is the time to complete the first four rectangles of (A).)

EXERCISES

A. Analyse the following in the way shown above:—

(i) A black and white dog jumped over the fence.
(ii) Under the mat lay a large envelope.
(iii) The runaway horse was careering down the main street.
(iv) After tea a tall man with a black beard will speak.
(v) Very few visitors have arrived.
(vi) Slowly but surely he crept towards the edge of the ravine.
(vii) The new centre-half played well.

(viii) No one had stayed behind to help with the washing-up.
(ix) You must not in these critical times behave recklessly.
(x) Every one in the class worked hard for the next week or two.

B. Construct sentences by adding an Adjective extension to the Subject and an Adverb extension to the Verb in:—

(i) batsman—played (which batsman? played how?)
(ii) invaders—landed (which invaders? landed when?)
(iii) sting—hurt
(iv) child—fell
(v) lorry—disappeared

CHAPTER III

THREE-ITEM BASIS: DIRECT OBJECT

Analyse:—

The tired soldier dropped into the ditch.

Now consider:—

The tired soldier dropped his rifle into the ditch.

Obviously 'soldier' and 'dropped' are basic items in both cases. But, whereas 'soldier dropped' is a fair summary of the first sentence, it does not fairly represent the second.

The 'dropped' in the first case concerns only the soldier. A Verb such as this, where the action is limited to the doer (i.e. its Subject), is INTRANSITIVE.

On the other hand, there are Verbs—TRANSITIVE VERBS—which denote actions which pass over, as it were, from one item to a *different* item. The first item is the Subject of the Verb, the second its DIRECT OBJECT. The pattern can be represented:—

SUBJECT	—V→	DIRECT OBJECT
I	hate	cheese
Hitler	declared	war

The basis of our second sentence is of this kind:—

soldier   dropped   rifle

The Direct Object, then, answers the question 'whom?' or 'what?' after a Transitive Verb and is a different person or thing from the Subject.

(*Note.*—Occasionally a Verb is used REFLEXIVELY: e.g. He shot himself. Here Subject and Direct Object denote the same person, but in the two separate senses of 'doer' and 'receiver'.)

The Direct Object is normally a Noun or Pronoun, and may therefore have an Adjectival extension. Hence our second sentence may be analysed:—

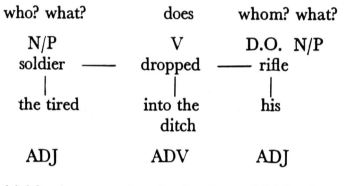

(See Chapter XXXI. Complete the first six rectangles of (B).)

EXERCISES

A. Remembering that not all Verbs take Direct Objects, analyse:—

(i) The delighted spectators threw their hats into the air.
(ii) A well-trained dog will not chase chickens.
(iii) In the excitement young Tom Jenkins slipped away from his father.
(iv) A machine-gun detachment attacked the pill-box in the wood.

28　　　PATTERN IN ENGLISH

- (v) 'Rubbish!' shouted a voice from the back of the hall.
- (vi) We listened quietly at the door for some minutes.
- (vii) Massive icebergs, white and menacing, threatened the little ship.
- (viii) My friend suddenly dived into the river.
- (ix) The infuriated beasts trampled their trainer to death.
- (x) Letter-writing always bored him terribly.

B. Some Verbs are by their nature always Transitive (e.g. 'to mention'): others are always Intransitive (e.g. 'to kneel'). Many can be used in either way, though in some cases one of the usages is very rare. For instance, 'dreamt' is (unusually) Transitive in 'I dreamt a strange dream last night'; whereas 'caught' is (unusually) Intransitive in 'The fish-hook caught in the seat of my trousers'.

Write sentences illustrating the Transitive use of: to stand, starve, sing, weep, talk—and the Intransitive use of: to ring, pass, wave, mix, carry.

C. Complete the following table:—

VERB	TRANSITIVE USE	INTRANSITIVE USE
thaw	The sun thawed the ice	The ice thawed
stop	The policeman stopped me	
blow		The hooter blew
write	She writes many letters	
bend		He bent over his victim

VERB	TRANSITIVE USE	INTRANSITIVE USE
stick	He stuck a patch over it	
move		Suddenly the table moved
keep	Many boys keep pets	
act		Betty often acts
wind	He wound a thread round the stick	

D. You need never confuse 'to lie' with 'to lay' if you remember that one of them is Transitive, the other Intransitive. Illustrate which is which by sentences, using the Verbs in various tenses and underlining the Direct Objects where appropriate.

E. 'Lay' and 'lie' are Transitive and Intransitive forms of the same word. 'To lay' means 'to cause to lie. Similarly, 'to fell' means 'to cause to fall'.

Do you know any other pairs of Verbs like these?

F. In representing the Transitive Verb pattern as Subject + V + Direct Object, we have considered only the sense in which 'a' does something to 'b'. This same action can be seen from the receiving end as:—

$$b \leftarrow V - a$$

These two ways of expressing the same circumstance are based on the ACTIVE and PASSIVE VOICES respectively of the Verb. For example:—

Active Voice: Tom struck Henry.
Passive Voice: Henry was struck by Tom.

Since it is nearly always with Transitive Verbs that the pattern can be so reversed, this is a useful test for identifying the Subject-Verb-Direct Object pattern.

Change the Voice of the Verbs in the following sentences:—

    (i) Joan beat Ruth at table tennis.
    (ii) The piano was played by a long-haired musician.
    (iii) The bazaar will be opened by the vicar's wife.
    (iv) Slugs have eaten all my seedlings.
    (v) Umbrellas are sometimes used by women as weapons.
    (vi) No-one could read his writing.
    (vii) Tobacco-growing needs a hot, wet climate.
    (viii) Cheque-books save time and trouble.
    (ix) The Jolly Roger was hoisted by the pirates.
    (x) His speech was received by the audience with jeers and catcalls.

G. Some Verbs otherwise usually Intransitive can take as Objects Nouns of kindred meaning to themselves. These Objects are called COGNATE OBJECTS:—

    Example: He *died* a painful *death*.

Construct similar sentences with the Verbs:—
live, sleep, dream, smile, laugh, weep, run, sigh, cough, look.

CHAPTER IV

THREE ITEM BASIS: SUBJECT-COMPLEMENT

Examine these pairs of sentences:—

    (*a*) Men eat animals.
        Men are animals.

    (*b*) He admired dictators.
        He became dictator.

    (*c*) It hurts me.
        It is I.

    (*d*) He avoids me.
        He seems unfriendly.

The first of each pair is of the pattern:—

$$\text{Subject} + \overrightarrow{\text{Verb}} + \text{Direct Object}.$$

The second of each pair has Subject + Verb, plus a third item which at first glance seems to answer the question 'what?'. But it is not a Direct Object, because:

    (i) The Verb denotes no action which passes over from one item to another different item: $(a \to b)$.
    (ii) The Verb cannot be made passive with the third item as Subject.

Verbs of this kind—mainly to be, become, seem, appear, feel, and Passive Verbs such as to be called, to be made—which are not Transitive and yet raise the question 'what?' are called VERBS of INCOMPLETE PREDICATION. The third item, which completes the Predication by saying something about the Subject, is called a SUBJECT COMPLEMENT.

This pattern may be represented:—

Subject + Verb + Subject-Complement.

There are two different kinds of Subject-Complement:—

(A)	(B)
He was a *pirate*.	He was *wicked*.
He became *president*.	He fell *ill*.
It was *he*.	It was *wet*.
He seemed a fine *sailor*.	He seemed remarkably *capable*.

Those under (A) are Nouns/Pronouns; those under (B) are Adjectives. Their extensions, if any, vary accordingly between the Adjective extension of a Noun/Pronoun (a *fine* sailor) and the Adverb extension of an Adjective (*remarkably* capable).

This difference is reflected in analysis:—

Example 1: The smallest boy may sometimes be the best player.

```
     N/P              V           S.C. N/P
     boy    —      may be    —     player
      |                |              |
 the smallest     sometimes       the best
     ADJ              ADV             ADJ
```

Example 2: The Christmas holidays seemed unbelievably short.

    N/P   V   S.C. ADJ
  holidays —   seemed —   short
     | |
the Christmas   unbelievably
    ADJ   ADV

(See Chapter XXXI. Complete the last pair of rectangles in Stencil (A).)

EXERCISES

A. We have distinguished between three types of Verb, or rather between three ways of using Verbs:—

(*a*) V.—the Intransitive Verb—e.g. sleeps.

(*b*) $\vec{V}$—the Transitive Verb—does, hits.

(*c*) $\bar{V}$—the Verb of Incomplete Predication—is.

The three corresponding patterns are:—

(*a*) Subject + Verb.

(*b*) Subject + $\vec{V}$erb + Direct Object.

(*c*) Subject + $\bar{V}$erb + Subject-Complement.

List the Finite Verbs in the following and indicate in which of these three ways each is used:—

It was a fine day when the model aeroplane display began. Many of the spectators had brought picnic baskets and had settled down to enjoy the demonstration. The children were in high spirits, though naturally the boys seemed more interested in the 'planes than the girls. The first flight took place promptly at eleven o'clock and set a high standard for the meeting. It soon became clear that some very high speeds would be reached.

B. List the Subject-Complements in the following sentences and indicate what part of speech each is:—

(i) I felt ashamed that I was so shabbily dressed.
(ii) He was vice-captain for several years before he at last became captain.
(iii) He was made foreman in due course, but was very unpopular with the men.
(iv) You will be sorry when I am dead and buried.
(v) I was not sure who was manager.

C. Analyse the following sentences, which contain Subject-Complements:—

(i) Obviously, the old man was quite exhausted.
(ii) Nobody seemed particularly pleased.
(iii) The old bull was usually called Brutus.
(iv) After a few days in bed the sick man felt much better.
(v) Without warning the mild breeze became a howling gale.
(vi) Any further attempt was considered too risky.
(vii) The only person present will be you.
(viii) The handle of this racquet feels very sticky.
(ix) The highwayman's accomplice had secretly turned informer.
(x) The large brown package was labelled on both sides 'Dangerous'.

D. Analyse:—

   (i) The old clock on the village hall always struck four at two o'clock.
   (ii) The main road was made impassable by the devastating floods.
   (iii) By nightfall the weather had considerably improved.
   (iv) Through the archway one could see a wide lawn.
   (v) Few people can write equally well with both hands.
   (vi) He might in more favourable circumstances have been a popular author.
   (vii) Without hesitation he threw his coat over the smouldering flames.
   (viii) An inexperienced punter had apparently fallen into the river.
   (ix) With the passing of time the wound grew less and less painful.
   (x) 'Heads!' called the opposing captain.

CHAPTER V

FOUR-ITEM BASIS: INDIRECT OBJECT

The basic pattern Subject + Verb + Subject-Complement does not admit of a fourth item. But a fourth item *is* possible with the pattern Subject + Verb + Direct Object.

Compare these two groups of sentences:—

A. 1. My mother bought a raincoat.
    2. The librarian gave a lecture on Kipling.
    3. At the cross-roads we asked the way.

B. 1. My mother bought *me* a raincoat.
    2. The librarian gave *the school* a lecture on Kipling.
    3. At the cross-roads we asked *a policeman* the way.

The basic pattern in Group A is Subject + Verb + Direct Object:—

	SUBJECT	VERB	DIRECT OBJECT
1.	mother	bought	raincoat
2.	librarian	gave	lecture
3.	we	asked	way

The same basic items are present and do the same work in the corresponding sentences in Group B. But there is also a fourth item, coming in each case between Verb and Direct Object. This item—me, the school, a policeman—is clearly not an extension. It resembles the Direct Object in that it seems to answer the question whom? or what? after the Verb and in that it can be made the Subject of a 'reversed' sentence:—

The school was given a lecture on Kipling by the librarian.

It is in fact an INDIRECT OBJECT. It is a Noun or Pronoun and may therefore have an Adjectival extension.

The Passive Voice reversal test (see page 29) often produces two possibilities in cases like this, according to which of the two Objects becomes Subject:—

Active Voice: My father gave the waitress a tip.
Passive Voice: The waitress was given a tip by my father.

OR

A tip was given to the waitress by my father.

Active Voice: My friend kept me a seat.
Passive Voice: I was kept a seat by my friend

OR

A seat was kept for me by my friend.

Whereas the Direct Object—a tip, a seat—stays the same in all three sentences, in the third sentence the Indirect Object—the waitress, me—becomes part of a word-group: *to* the waitress, *for* me.

The idea to/for was in fact present from the beginning. The original sentences correspond in meaning closely, though not exactly, to:—

My father gave a tip *to* the waitress.
My friend kept a seat *for* me.

Notice, however, that the order of the items changes when these word-groups are put in place of the Indirect Objects. It is only when the to/for notion is not expressed but merely understood that the Indirect Object is used, taking its place between Verb and Direct Object. (See also page 81 on the 'to'-phrase.)

The pattern, then, is:—

SUBJECT	VERB	INDIRECT OBJECT	DIRECT OBJECT
who? what?	does	(to/for) whom? what?	whom? what?

A fully analysed example would be:—

This week many shops are offering their customers unusually cheap bargains.

```
      N/P            V       I.O. N/P   D.O. N/P
      shops—are offering—customers—bargains
        |            |          |          |
      many       this week    their    unusually
                                          cheap
       ADJ          ADV        ADJ        ADJ
```

Only a limited number of Verbs can take an Indirect as well as a Direct Object. The commonest are:—

> to give, present, offer, send—and Verbs of similar meaning.

Notice that, though it is common enough to have a Direct without an Indirect Object, it is impossible to have the Indirect Object alone.

(See Chapter XXXI. Complete Stencil (C).)

EXERCISES

A. Analyse the following sentences:—

(i) The man next door offered me a cigarette.
(ii) The old sailor told the holidaymakers a long sea story.
(iii) An injection of morphia brought temporary relief from the pain.
(iv) The kindly landlady brought her guests bacon and eggs in bed.
(v) A disused cowshed afforded us shelter from the storm.
(vi) We lit a fire in the corner.
(vii) The negro boxer dealt his opponent a heavy blow in the stomach.
(viii) The van stopped at the end of the street.
(ix) You should ask your father his views on the matter.
(x) Last year the firm sent each employee a cheque for ten pounds.

B. Analyse:—

(i) A strange animal had been found on the sea-shore.
(ii) It seemed quite dead.
(iii) An inquisitive soldier gave it a prod with a stick.
(iv) For a few minutes nothing happened.
(v) Then the creature uttered a low moaning sound.
(vi) The noise was indescribably weird.
(vii) A little later the local policeman arrived.

(viii) The soldier told him the details of the discovery.
(ix) The conscientious policeman wrote a long report in his notebook.
(x) By this time the animal had become a lifeless hulk.

C. Write sentences containing the following items (in rearranged order) and underline the Indirect Objects:—

(i) centre-forward—ball—kick—gave
(ii) shorthand—aunt—her—taught
(iii) newspaper—brought—dog—master
(iv) made—promise—mother—boy
(v) made—cocoa—himself—night-watchman

D. Rewrite the following sentences, using Indirect Objects instead of the words in italics:—

(i) Please send a copy of the local paper *to me* each week.
(ii) The lecturer showed some photographs of the Himalayas *to his audience*.
(iii) Fetch a glass of brandy *for the injured man*.
(iv) They waved an excited welcome *to the Channel swimmer*.
(v) The newly promoted bank manager bought a fur coat *for his wife*.

CHAPTER VI

FOUR-ITEM BASIS: OBJECT-COMPLEMENT

The Indirect Object is not the only fourth item possible with Subject + Verb + Direct Object.

Examine the following pairs of sentences:—

The election was declared *invalid*.
The committee declared the election *invalid*.

Jones seems *a genius*.
I consider Jones *a genius*.

He was made *bad-tempered* by gout.
Gout made him *bad-tempered*.

The first of each pair, with the Subject-Complement in italics, is of the pattern:—

Subject + Verb + Subject-Complement.

In the second of each pair the italicised word is used after the pattern:—

Subject + Verb + Direct Object.

In each pair of sentences the italicised word 'completes' a statement about the same person or thing (election, Jones, he/him), but the person or thing is a Subject in the first instance, a Direct Object in the second. We have, therefore, in the second case, to deal with an OBJECT-COMPLEMENT.

The two kinds of Complement are very similar. They both follow the so-called Verbs of Incomplete Predication. In fact, the notion 'to be' is usually present with both types.

The Verbs commonly followed by Subject-Complements are, in addition to 'to be' itself:—

to become	(to come *to be*)
to seem, appear	(to look *to be*)
to be called	(to be said *to be*)

The Verbs commonly followed by Object-Complements are:—

to make, elect, choose	(to cause *to be*),
to consider	(to think *to be*),
to call	(to say *to be*).

The Object-Complement, like the Subject-Complement, may be either a Noun/Pronoun or an Adjective, with a possible Adjective or Adverb extension respectively:—

(*a*) The angry master called the boy a stupid blockhead.

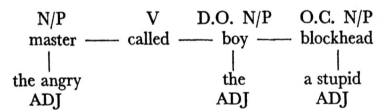

(*b*) In your sketch you have drawn the thatched cottage distinctly lop-sided.

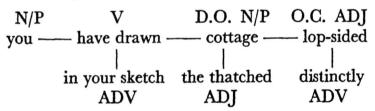

(See Chapter XXXI. Complete the last pair of rectangles in Stencil (B).)

EXERCISES

A. Analyse the following sentences, which contain Object-Complements:—

    (i) The incessant noise nearly drove him mad.
    (ii) The four judges unanimously appointed the youngest girl Beauty Queen of Margate.
    (iii) He used to think himself very popular.
    (iv) His long illness had made him extremely irritable.
    (v) Princess Edwina then named the new vessel the 'Catriona'.
    (vi) The rolling of the boat soon turned his face green.
    (vii) We consider it scandalous.
    (viii) The victorious general made the capital city his new headquarters.
    (ix) His friends always call him 'Basher'.
    (x) The new officer showed himself thoroughly efficient.

B. The Subject + Verb + Subject-Complement pattern with a Passive Verb (see page 31) can often be turned into a corresponding Active Voice pattern of Subject + Verb + Direct Object + Object-Complement, e.g.:—

    He was made secretary.
    They made him secretary.

Do likewise with the following sentences:—

    (i) Briggs was thought by everybody to be crazy.
    (ii) He was called 'Dopey' by all the children.
    (iii) His life was made intolerable by a nagging wife.

44 PATTERN IN ENGLISH

    (iv) He was considered a genius by his parents.
    (v) The statue had been painted red by a practical joker.

C. Construct sentences containing the following items (not in this order) and underline the Object-Complements:—

    (i) Eskimo—found—unbearable—heat
    (ii) Shaw—consider—people—writer
    (iii) surgery—drawing-room—made—doctor
    (iv) artist—pink—sea—painted
    (v) has made—perfect—him—practice.

D. Analyse:—

    (i) Every night the lodger read the evening paper from cover to cover.
    (ii) An old friend has written me a long letter from China.
    (iii) My typewriter has proved a most useful instrument.
    (iv) The flags hung listlessly in the still air.
    (v) The town band repeatedly played a doleful march.
    (vi) The old earl was made furious by his daughter's unseemly behaviour.
    (vii) His wife's attitude made him even angrier.
    (viii) The postman has not brought us any letters for days.
    (ix) An ancient piano occasionally sounded from the next room.
    (x) The garrison commander unexpectedly nominated Lieutenant Jones his chief of staff.

CHAPTER VII

WORD-ORDER: COMMANDS, QUESTIONS, EXCLAMATIONS

We have examined five basic patterns:—

Subj. + Verb.
Subj. + Verb + D. Obj.
Subj. + Verb + Subj.-Comp.
Subj. + Verb + Ind. Obj. + D. Obj.
Subj. + Verb + D. Obj. + Obj.-Comp.

These show clearly that the normal order of items in English is:—

1. Subject.
2. Verb.
3. Objects and/or Complements.

(We notice also that the Indirect Object precedes the Direct Object, but the Object-Complement follows it.)

This standard order is, of course, not unchangeable. For the sake of variety, emphasis and other effects of style it is often changed.

We have already noticed (page 12) how the Verb may sometimes precede its Subject:—

Round the corner *came an errand boy* on a bicycle.

A less common variant is the order:—

Object or Complement + Subject + Verb.

Examples:—

A strange man he was.
His money he kept in a grand piano.

Sometimes the normal order is completely reversed into:—

Object or Complement + Verb + Subject.

With the Object this reversal is not often possible without risking misunderstanding (Why?), but it is useful in handling short speeches:—

'Shoot!' screamed the excited spectators.

With the Complement the reversal is effective if used sparingly:—

A remarkable man was Alexander Kinglake.

It is advisable to use the normal order of Subject + Verb + Object or Complement regularly, except when there is a special reason for departing from it.

Sometimes it is the standard order alone that determines the meaning intended:—

Compare—The First Infantry Brigade attacked the enemy
with — The enemy attacked the First Infantry Brigade.

In cases like these we take it for granted that the preceding Noun/Pronoun is the Subject and the following Noun/Pronoun the Direct Object of the Verb.

It is convenient at this stage to consider Simple Sentences which are not statements, since these—Commands, Questions and Exclamations—in many cases depart from the normal order of items.

COMMANDS

The main mark of a *spoken* command or instruction is the speech rhythm and tone of voice. In *writing* the chief indication is the lack of a stated Subject. The adding of the understood 'you' usually produces a Statement that can readily be analysed:—

    Bring me a class of water.

N/P	V	I.O. N/P	D.O. N/P
(you)	— bring —	me —	glass
			|
			a ... of
			water
			ADJ

QUESTIONS

(*a*) Sometimes the questioning tone of voice or the written question-mark is the only clue:—

    You remembered to post my letter?

This is not strictly a matter of grammar at all.

(*b*) The type of question which calls for a Yes or No answer is often expressed merely by a change in word-order from the corresponding statement:—

STATEMENT	QUESTION
It is raining.	Is it raining?
The result was satisfactory.	Was the result satisfactory?

Analysis will not reflect this difference:—

N/P	V, etc.
it	— is raining
the result	— was satisfactory

(c) The splitting of the Verb into two parts, with the Subject in the middle (Is *it* raining?), is typical of this type of question. Where the Verb in the corresponding statement is a single word it is usually changed in the Question into a Verb of more than one word, to make the splitting possible. Hence:—

    STATEMENT   QUESTION

    You did it.   *Did* you *do* it?

Analysis treats the Question like the Statement:—

N/P	V	D.O. N/P
you —	did do	— it

(d) Questions requiring answers other than Yes or No normally begin with a suitable questioning word —Interrogative Pronoun or Adverb—such as who?, what?, how?, when?, why? In the analysis it is best to treat these little words in the same way as the corresponding items in the answers to the questions:—

Why did you do it?

N/P	V	DO. N/P
you —	did do	— it
	|	
	why	
	ADV	

EXCLAMATIONS

Similarly, Exclamations should be analysed as if they were the corresponding statements:—

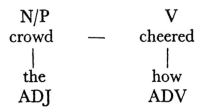

This does not make much sense. That is because Exclamations are concerned less with sense than with feelings. The simplest Exclamations are merely noises. (Oh! Tut, tut!) Words like these are called INTER-JECTIONS.

EXERCISES

A. Analyse the following sentences:—

   (i) How well you look!
   (ii) Have you been visiting the doctor?
   (iii) Wipe your boots on the mat before entering.
   (iv) Did she learn shorthand at school?
   (v) Take his temperature every four hours.
   (vi) Were you made a chief scout very long ago?
   (vii) What a disappointment the whole wretched business has been!
   (viii) What on earth did you do that for?
   (ix) Be careful with that gun.
   (x) Give the boy his cricket bat immediately.

B. Construct sentences on the following basic patterns, with extensions where needed:—

   (i) Verb + Subject.
   (ii) Direct Object + Subject + Verb.
   (iii) Direct Object + Verb + Subject.
   (iv) Subject-Complement + Subject + Verb.
   (v) Subject-Complement + Verb + Subject.

CHAPTER VIII
CASE

It is convenient here to notice that the Nouns and Pronouns which figure so largely in our patterns are said to be in different CASES according to the different jobs they do:—

(*a*) The Subject or Subject-Complement is in the NOMINATIVE Case.

(*b*) The Object or Object-Complement is in the OBJECTIVE Case.

Note.—Students of foreign languages may distinguish between two Objective Cases: the Accusative of the Direct Object and the Dative of the Indirect Object.

In Old English, Nouns and Pronouns were spelt differently in these and other Cases. The various endings have since disappeared from Nouns, but Pronouns have kept some variations:—

	SINGULAR	PLURAL
Nominative:	I he who	we they
Objective:	me him whom	us them

There is another Case—the POSSESSIVE or GENITIVE —which has kept its special spelling with Nouns as well as Pronouns.

To show possession we have the Possessive Pronouns: mine, ours, yours, his, its, hers, theirs, whose.

The Possessive Case of Nouns is formed by adding 's to the Nominative (Singular or Plural), except when that sounds ugly. In the latter case no change is made in speech, though the simple apostrophe (') is added in writing:—

	NOMINATIVE	POSSESSIVE
Singular	man	man's
Plural	men	men's
Singular	boy	boy's
Plural	boys	boys'

Sometimes it is a matter of taste. One can say either 'Jones' house' or 'Jones's house'.

Notes.—(*a*) Beware of confusing this apostrophe of possession with the apostrophe of omission (it's = it is; don't = do not, etc.).

(*b*) The Possessive Case is not the only way of indicating possession. It is very common where the possessor is a person or is thought of personally (A blast on the *ship's* siren indicated *her* approach), but with things it is much less common than an 'of'-construction (the top of the table, the end of the street). Sometimes either phrasing is possible (the book's title, the title of the book), but there is often a difference of meaning between the two. 'The construction of a house' is not quite the same as 'A house's construction'. (See also Preposition-Phrases, pages 72–75.)

EXERCISES

A. Explain and correct the mistakes in the following:
  (i) Dad took Mum and I for a row round the harbour.

(ii) Between you and I, Dick is not playing so well as at the beginning of the season.
(iii) The constable wrote down each boys' name and address.
(iv) Their garden is much longer, than our's.
(v) "E gave I a dirty look and pushed I into the river.'
(vi) I do not know whom it could have been.
(vii) The river has overflowed it's banks.
(viii) 'It's a skylark', thought John, as he listened to its shrill song and admired it's hovering.
(ix) He was wearing a suit of mens' overalls.
(x) My two cousins, my sister and me set out early next morning.

B. Rewrite the following, using Nouns in the Possessive Case in place of the word-groups in italics:—

Example: Encyclopedia *for children*.
Children's encyclopedia.

(i) Bottom was wearing the head *of an ass*.
(ii) The shoes *of ladies* are often high-heeled.
(iii) Henry VIII showed little consideration for the feelings *of his wives*.
(iv) American trains have separate compartments *for negroes*.
(v) Macbeth was impressed by the prophecies *of the witches*.

PART TWO
EQUIVALENTS

CHAPTER IX

WORD, PHRASE AND CLAUSE

Simple Sentences, we have seen, are arrangements of items into patterns. The important thing about each item is the work it does in relation to the other items—that is, its function.

But we have also noticed how the various functions are usually performed by certain Parts of Speech rather than others: Subjects and Objects are normally Nouns or Pronouns; Complements are normally Nouns, Pronouns or Adjectives; Extensions of Nouns and Pronouns are normally Adjectives; Extensions of Verbs and Adjectives are normally Adverbs.

Make a list of the basic Subject words in the following sentences:—

> Bernard Shaw is a remarkable playwright.
> He has written very many plays.
> Writing comes easily to him.
> His longest play is ' Man and Superman'.
> His best is 'Saint Joan'.
> Some are more interesting than others.
> Few are more popular than 'Pygmalion'.
> Old and young enjoy this last play.

Now forget these sentences for a moment and examine your list of single words. What Part of Speech does each seem to be? Does not the list include Adjectives (e.g. old, best) and a Verb (writing) in addition to the Nouns and Pronouns you might expect?

It does. Just as Pronouns commonly represent Nouns ('He' in the second sentence above stands for 'Shaw'), so in certain circumstances other Parts of Speech (Adjectives and -ing Verbs, for instance) do the jobs normally performed by Nouns.

In other words, the Noun-Functions (Subject, Object, Complement) are usually performed by Nouns, but may also be performed by other Parts of Speech. Similarly, the Adverb-Functions (extending Verbs, Adjectives or Adverbs) may on occasion be performed by words other than Adverbs (e.g. an Infinitive Verb in 'He sat down *to relax*'). And so on.

When a word which is normally one Part of Speech does the work of another it is for that occasion EQUIVALENT to that second Part of Speech.

EXERCISE

Explain how, in the following sentences, each word in italics, though normally regarded as one Part of Speech, is here equivalent to another.

Example: A *pistol* shot rang out. (Noun equivalent to Adjective.)

    (i) He gave his money to the *poor*.
   (ii) *Talking* is forbidden.
  (iii) Their best plan was *to retreat*.

(iv) They knelt down *to pray*.
(v) He found the machine *broken*.

* * *

Another kind of Equivalent is a word-group which does the work of a single word:—

He swore that he would not *put up with* it. (Compare: . . . he would not tolerate it.)

He joined the Army *of his own accord*. (Compare . . . voluntarily.)

Such word-groups, which may be treated as single items, are called PHRASES.

The Phrase may or may not include the Part of Speech to which it, as a unit, is equivalent. The Verb-Equivalent 'fell down' includes the Verb 'fell'; the Adjective Phrase 'with long, red hair' contains the Adjectives 'long' and 'red'. But there is no Adverb in the Adverb-Equivalent 'in the middle of the road'.

EXERCISE

Pick out the Phrases in the following and say to what Part of Speech each is equivalent:—

(i) He dived into the swimming pool.
(ii) The professor took off his gown.
(iii) It was a matter of some importance.
(iv) He saw a strange figure drawing near.
(v) She wore gloves lined with fur.

* * *

Besides the single word and the Phrase there is a third equivalent, the CLAUSE. This is a word-group which contains its own Predication (Subject + Finite Verb).

Clauses vary in importance from (*a*) the near-phrase which happens to have the Finite Verb instead of Participle:—

The man *who was sitting next to me* coughed. (Clause.)
The man *sitting next to me* coughed. (Phrase.)

—to (*b*) the near-sentence:—

The ice, *which was very thin*, made skating risky. (Clause.)
The ice was very thin. It made skating risky. (Sentence.)

For the sake of completeness we shall briefly mention Clauses in connection with the various classes of Equivalent, but, since they bring us to sentences with more than one Predication—i.e. not Simple Sentences—we shall reserve fuller treatment of them until later. (See Part IV—Multiple Sentences.)

The chief Equivalents, which we shall examine in turn, are:—

Part of Speech	Equivalents	Examples	See Pages
Verb.	Compound Verb.	He *ran over* the line.	58–61
Noun.	Pronoun.	he, us, theirs, whom, one	62–65
	Verb-Noun, including Gerund	*Seeing* is *believing*.	65–67
	Infinitive.	*To know* all is *to forgive* all.	
	Adjective.	The *last* shall be first.	67
	Noun Clause.	He forgot *that the shops were closed*	67–68

Part of Speech	Equivalents	Examples	See Pages
Adjective.	Verb-Adjective, including		69–71
	Present Participle	The result was *encouraging*.	
	Past Participle.	*Exhausted*, he struggled on.	
	Preposition-Phrase.	It was *of no avail*.	71–74
	Noun.	A *music* stand.	74–76
	Infinitive.	Bring something *to drink*.	76–77
	Adjective Clause.	I prefer films *that amuse*.	77
Adverb.	Infinitive.	He came *to see me*.	79–80
	Preposition-Phrase.	He disappeared *round the corner*.	80–83
	Adverb Clause.	The storm died down *as night fell*.	83

Note.—Verb-Nouns and Verb-Adjectives, while acting as Nouns and Adjectives, often retain enough of their Verb quality to have their own Objects, Complements and Extensions. In such cases the whole phrase should be treated as an Equivalent:—

Exhausted by his vain efforts to reach his companion, he collapsed in the snow.

CHAPTER X

VERB-EQUIVALENTS

Examine the items in italics:—

Before deciding to buy the house, he *looked over it* thoroughly. He even *looked over the wall* into the garden next door.

The two uses are quite different. The second sentence could be analysed:—

N/P	V
He —	looked
	|
	over the wall, etc.
	ADV
	where?

But the basis of the first sentence must be:—

N/P	V	D.O. N/P
He —	looked over —	it

Here the phrase 'looked over' is equivalent to a single Verb; it corresponds to 'inspected' or 'examined'. This COMPOUND VERB, as it is called, is very common. It consists of a Verb plus an Adverb or Preposition. But Verb + Adverb or Preposition = Compound Verb only when they are thought of as a single action. Each case must therefore be decided separately.

Sometimes it is impossible to decide finally one way or the other. For example:—

He rushed at his opponent.

This can be read either as:—

> He rushed-at (i.e. attacked) his opponent.
> Subject + Verb-Equivalent + Direct Object,

or as:—

> He rushed at-his-opponent.
> Subject + Verb + Adverb Phrase of Place.

Sometimes the true Verb-Equivalent can be distinguished because it can be turned into the Passive Voice:—

> He locked up the office.
> The office was locked up by him.

Such a reversal is impossible with the Adverb Phrase:—

> He looked towards the church.

EXERCISES

A. Analyse:—
  (i) Pull up your socks.
  (ii) The old sailor looked at the strange vessel through his telescope.
  (iii) The burning plane crashed into the sea.
  (iv) Will you come with me to the circus tomorrow night?
  (v) He covered up the blot with a piece of paper just in time.
  (vi) The commissionaire rushed up the stairs six at a time.
  (vii) Think of the disgrace!
  (viii) The farmers are all praying for rain.

(ix) After school he went directly to the headmaster's study.
(x) The dentist took out five of his patient's front teeth.

B. Complete the following table:—

COMPOUND VERB		SIMPLE VERB
to go up	=	to ascend
to wait for	=	
	=	to demand
	=	to deride
to wish for	=	
to wait upon	=	
	=	to consider
to speak of	=	
to go to	=	
	=	to remove

C. Example:—

I waited for-ten-minutes.
I waited-for the next bus.

Write similar pairs of sentences based on the following:—

| to take up | to run down | to wait on |
| to look for | to deal with | |

D. Examine the word 'open' in: He pushed the door *open*. It might be considered either as part of the Compound Verb (He *pushed-open* the door = He *opened* the door) or as an Adjective acting as Object-Complement (i.e. He *caused* the door *to be* open).

Cases like these are arguable. In which of the following do you find a Compound Verb:—

    (i) We set the craft afloat on the lake.
   (ii) The referee broke the boxers apart.
  (iii) They threw the carcase overboard.
  (iv) The cold spell has frozen the ice hard.
   (v) He painted the house red.
  (vi) The captain brought the ship alongside.
 (vii) The plough turned the soil over.
(viii) Bring the lamp down.
  (ix) Constant use had worn the surface smooth.
   (x) His infinite patience carried him through.

CHAPTER XI

NOUN-EQUIVALENTS

Noun-equivalents include:—

(*a*) Pronouns.
(*b*) Verb-Nouns (Gerunds and Infinitives)—alone or as part of Noun Phrases.
(*c*) Adjectives.
(*d*) Noun Clauses.

PRONOUNS are very common substitutes for Nouns. Their purpose is to save the reader or listener from the tedious repetition of Nouns. This purpose is defeated if it is not immediately clear which Noun each Pronoun stands for.

Here are some of the ways in which Pronouns are often misused:—

1. In a public library a person can find a book *they* want.
    Note.—A Pronoun must agree in Number with the Noun it represents. A Plural Pronoun ('they') cannot stand for a Singular Noun ('person').
2. Portia and Nerissa disguise themselves as men and go to the court. *She* says that Bellario has sent her.
    Note.—A Singular Pronoun should refer back to one separate Singular Noun, not to one part of a dual item.
3. People also like libraries because *you* can borrow books of all kinds from them.

Note.—A Pronoun must agree in Person with the Noun it represents. A Second Person Pronoun ('you') cannot stand for a Third Person Noun ('People').

4. When the kettle is boiling, pour *it* into the teapot and stir *it* up.

Note.—A Pronoun must refer back to a recently stated Noun. It should not relate to an implied but unstated Noun ('water'), especially when another Noun ('kettle') is involved.

EXERCISES

A. Correct the above faulty sentences.
B. Explain and correct the faults in:—
  (i) Boys start collections merely as an excuse to do something he ought not to do.
  (ii) A short time ago most Swiss people worked on the land, but this could only be done in the northern part of Switzerland.
  (iii) A tent is useful to circus owners because they can be moved about.
  (iv) The spikes on the tractor wheels sink into the ground and stop it from slipping.
  (v) Horses have four legs and a tail, and it stands about six feet above the ground when it is fully grown.
  (vi) Shylock and Antonio agreed that, if he did not repay the loan within three months, he should forfeit a pound of his flesh.
  (vii) When one is tired of life, you should find some work to do.
  (viii) When you have found the hole, sandpaper it carefully.

(ix) Film is highly inflammable; they should therefore be kept cool.

(x) A helicopter has special advantages, because they can hover in the air.

* * *

The Pronoun 'it' (and the pseudo-Pronoun 'there') are often used as PROVISIONAL SUBJECTS or OBJECTS, in various ways:—

(*a*) The Pronoun 'it' is commonly used as a makeshift Subject, the real Subject being stated later in the sentence, e.g.:—

It is difficult to sleep standing up.

The real Subject—'to sleep standing up'—is too long to read comfortably in front of the Verb.

(*b*) A similar construction is frequent where the real Subject is a Noun Clause (see page 117). Instead of clumsily preceding the Verb (e.g. *That he would resign was expected*), the Clause is used in Apposition to an acting Subject 'it':—

It was expected that he would resign.

(*c*) A Noun Clause may be used as the Subject-Complement of a nominal Subject 'it':—

It was in 1892 that Gladstone made his famous speech.

(*d*) The Provisional Object followed by an Object-Complement which represents the real Object is also common:—

He thought *it* unlikely that snow would fall.

(*e*) In statements like '*It* is raining' the real Subject is indefinable, and 'it' is used in its place.

(*f*) 'There' is sometimes used as a Provisional Subject:—

There lived on the island an old hermit.

EXERCISE

Rewrite the following sentences, using 'it' as a Provisional Subject in each case:—

(i) To advance further meant certain death.
(ii) That the Rangers would win the Cup seemed a certainty.
(iii) Shakespeare wrote his finest tragedies during James I's reign.
(iv) That John was telling the whole truth was doubtful.
(v) To use the front gate was forbidden.

* * *

VERB-NOUNS. A Verb denotes action or being; a Noun names a person or thing. If the thing named be an action, the two functions are mixed:—

SUBJECT	PREDICATE
(*a*) Cookery	is a science.
(*b*) Cooking	is warm work.
(*c*) To cook	is easier than to cook well.

'Cooking' and 'to cook' are both non-Finite parts of the Verb. The Verb-Noun in '-ing' is called a GERUND. (It is liable to be confused with the Verb-Adjective '-ing' form called the Present Participle—see page 69).

The Verb-Noun 'to . . .' is called an INFINITIVE.
Like ordinary Nouns, these Verb-Nouns can also be used as Objects and Complements:—

Object: He liked *fishing*.
I preferred *to swim*.
Complement: My favourite recreation is *rowing*.
Her intention was *to emigrate*.

Taking the term 'Noun' to include Noun-Equivalents, the analysis is straightforward:—

N/P	V	S.C. N/P
seeing	— is —	believing

A Verb-Noun, while doing the work of a Noun, may remain enough of a Verb to be followed by an Object or Complement or Adverb extension. For our purpose these extra items should stay with their Verb-Nouns:—

N/P	V	S.C. N/P
Feeding the bears with doughnuts	— is —	forbidden

Certain Verbs seem to take two Direct Objects, of which the second is an Infinitive (usually without 'to') equivalent to a Noun:—

Let me *go*.
I saw the boat *sink*.

Similar constructions are possible after Verbs like 'allow', 'hear'.

EXERCISE

Example:—

> Thorough *preparation* ensures success.
> He hated *preparing* for examinations.
> He refused *to prepare* his lessons.

Write similar trios of sentences based on the following Nouns and Noun-Equivalents, using them in any position and with or without Objects, etc.:—

(i) composition   composing   to compose
(ii) sight   seeing   to see
(iii) trial   trying   to try
(iv) revision   revising   to revise
(v) growth   growing   to grow

*   *   *

ADJECTIVES, usually but not always with 'the', may be used as Nouns:—

> Blessed are *the meek*.
> *The long* and *the short* of it was that the game was up.
> *Old* and *young*, *strong* and *weak*, *lame* and *healthy*, all helped in the evacuation.

Present Participles (i.e. Verb-Adjectives—see page 69) can be used similarly:—

> *The dying* outnumbered *the living*; *the slain* outnumbered *the wounded*.

NOUN CLAUSES, as we shall see in more detail later (Chapter XX) are equivalent to Nouns, and may carry out any of their functions. One example will suffice here:—

Compare: He noticed *that changes had been made*
(Noun Clause)
with: He noticed alterations. (Noun.)

EXERCISES

A. After analysing the following sentences, pick out the Noun-Equivalents and state what kind each is:—

(i) For some months he had been thinking of resigning.
(ii) Man had for centuries been trying to fly.
(iii) He gave the needy food and clothing.
(iv) To tease a lion is asking for trouble.
(v) Constant sunbathing had turned his skin dark brown.
(vi) Only the brave deserve the fair.
(vii) He gave stamp-collecting much of his time.
(viii) To travel hopefully is better than to arrive.
(ix) At the nets the cricket coach picked out the ten most efficient.
(x) Rehearsing comes before acting.

B. Example: *Dead* men tell no tales. (Adjective.)
Ghosts walk in the *dead* of night.
(Adjective as Noun-Equivalent.)

Write pairs of sentences using the following Adjectives similarly:—

poor, good, many, few, elderly.

CHAPTER XII

ADJECTIVE-EQUIVALENTS

Adjective-Equivalents fall into five classes:—
(*a*) Participles and Participial Phrases.
(*b*) Preposition-Phrases.
(*c*) Nouns.
(*d*) The Infinitive.
(*e*) Adjective Clauses.

PARTICIPLES AND PARTICIPIAL PHRASES

The main forms of the Verb are:—

		Functions mainly as:—
VERB	Finite Verb	broke — Verb
	Infinitive	to break ⎫
	Gerund	breaking ⎬ Noun
	Participles	breaking ⎫
		broken ⎬ Adjective

Just as Verb-Nouns seem sometimes more Verb than Noun, at other times more Noun than Verb, so Verb-Adjectives vary in character between near-Verbs and near-Adjectives.

The PRESENT PARTICIPLE in '*walking*-stick' and the PAST PARTICIPLE in '*jugged* hare' are both almost complete Adjectives. On the other hand, the Participles often show their Verbal nature by taking Objects, Complements and Adverb extensions, thus forming ADJECTIVE-PHRASES.

Whereas the Noun or Noun-Phrase normally belongs to the basis of the Simple Sentence, the Adjective or

Adjective-Phrase may belong either to the basis (as an Adjective Complement) or to the extensions (extending a Noun or Pronoun):—

Examples:—

(a) The heat was *overpowering*.

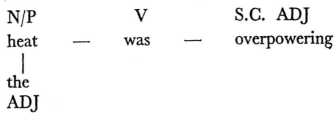

(b) *Swiftly picking up his belongings,* he strode away.

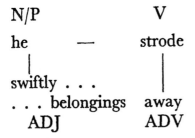

Note.—The Present Participle has an Active sense (i.e. it indicates 'doing' an action). The Past Participle has a Passive sense (i.e. it indicates 'receiving' or 'suffering' an action). (See page 29 on Voice.)

(c) *Overcome by remorse,* he picked up the violin *smashed beyond repair.*

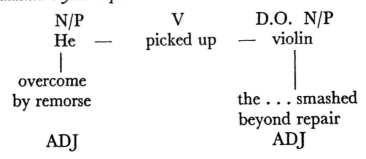

EXERCISES

A. Analyse the following sentences and describe the Adjective-Equivalents, indicating, for instance, whether they are Extensions or Complements, Participles or Participial Phrases, Present or Past:—

(i) A howling gale sprang up during the night.
(ii) He seemed pleased with himself.
(iii) Living all alone, the old woman had become quite eccentric.
(iv) The door remained locked.
(v) The cliff, undermined by the exceptional tides, suddenly crumbled.
(vi) He seemed bursting with energy.
(vii) The experience was most disturbing.
(viii) The fox, trapped, turned to face its enemies.
(ix) His strange behaviour made him distrusted by everybody.
(x) The judge considered the witness's answers irritating.

B. Where possible, substitute in the above sentences alternative Adjectives or Adjective-Equivalents. For example:—

(i) A *fierce* gale sprang up . . . (Simple Adjective).
A gale, *heralding the approach of winter*, sprang up . . . (Present Participial Phrase equivalent to Adjective).

* * *

It is easier to recognise a PREPOSITION–PHRASE than to describe it. Here are some examples:—

In the long overcoat	with a beard
to no purpose	for young children

(a book) on swimming   beyond the horizon
    under the circumstances above suspicion
    at considerable expense of Charles Dickens

These Phrases run to a pattern of two items. The second item is a Noun or Noun-Equivalent (overcoat, beard, purpose, children, swimming), with perhaps an Adjective extension (a long, a, no, young).

The first item is a PREPOSITION, so called because it is placed before (Latin *prae-positus*) a Noun or Noun-Equivalent.

The Preposition shows a relationship between the Noun it 'governs' and some other item. This relationship may be one of many kinds. It may indicate the Place or Manner of an action or happening, for instance. In this case it is an Adverb-Equivalent. (See page 81.)

On the other hand, the relationship may be in some way descriptive, the 'other item' being a Noun/Pronoun. In this case the phrase is an Adjective-Equivalent.

Example: Which man? The man *in the long overcoat*.

The Preposition 'in' connects 'long overcoat' with 'man', so describing him. The Phrase 'in the long overcoat' is therefore an Adjective-Equivalent.

Once again, the Adjective-Equivalent may carry out either of the functions of an Adjective. It can act as Complement or as extension of a Noun/Pronoun.

Examples: (*a*) The judge considered the evidence *out of order*.

N/P   V   D.O. N/P   O.C. ADJ
judge — considered — evidence — out of order
  | |
the   the

(b) The man *with the limp* was following the officer *in naval uniform*.

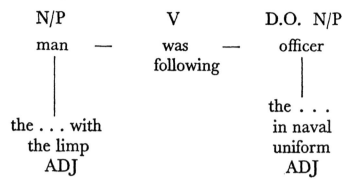

Note.—Sometimes the relationship is so obvious that the Preposition is not actually stated, but left understood. This is particularly so in the case of 'with':—

(With) Cap in hand, he stood humbly before the duke.

EXERCISES

A. Find the Preposition-Phrases equivalent to Adjectives in the following sentences. (Analyse the sentences first, if necessary.) Describe them, indicating, for instance, whether they are Extensions or Complements:—

(i) The man from the insurance company called this morning.
(ii) Their house was in a dilapidated condition.
(iii) I have never read a book with such a strange ending.
(iv) The bank declared the notes out of date.
(v) The headmaster appointed Jones captain of the school.
(vi) The treasurer was elected chairman for the time being.

(vii) The police searched the house at the corner.
(viii) An empty space behind the cycle-shed is for sale.
(ix) The Town Council gave all children without parents Christmas presents.
(x) Heavy storms had left the grass near the goalposts under water.

B. Where possible rewrite the sentences in Exercise A above, using single Adjectives instead of the Preposition-Phrases (and making any slight alterations necessary).

Example: (x) Heavy storms had left the goal areas *waterlogged*.

C. Rewrite the following sentences, substituting Preposition-Phrases for Participle-Phrases and vice versa (and making any slight alterations that become necessary).

Example: The pirate chief, *raging furiously*, swore that he would get his revenge.
The pirate chief, *in a furious rage*, swore that . . .

(i) A mechanic holding a spanner was standing nearby.
(ii) A letter in neat handwriting came next day.
(iii) All police patrols were instructed to look out for a tall dark man at the wheel of an Austin Seven.
(iv) He noticed a heavily built foreigner limping very badly.
(v) A small boy, covered with mud, approached me.

* * *

NOUNS as Adjective-Equivalents. Nouns (and

Verb-Nouns used as Adjectives) often correspond to Preposition-Phrases:—

Noun as Adjective	Preposition-Phrase
a *ball* game	a game *with a ball*
a *shaving* brush	a brush *for shaving*
Scott's novels	the novels *of Scott*
hailstones *the size* of oranges	hailstones *of the size of* oranges

Sometimes, however, the Noun as Adjective is merely placed next to the Noun it qualifies, i.e. in Apposition to it:—

You *Americans*.
Prince John, *Regent* of England.

EXERCISES

A. Example: He cut his throat with a *razor*.

Razor blades are dangerous things.

Write pairs of sentences in which the following words are used firstly as simple Nouns and then as Adjective-equivalents:—

prize, remembrance, Channel, step, book, golf, Diesel, film, key, Gladstone.

B. Example: He spent the rest of his life in the cell of a *prison*. (Noun as Adjective.)
He spent the rest of his life in a *prison cell*.

Rewrite the following sentences, substituting for the word(s) in italics the kind of Adjective-Equivalent indicated:—

- (i) Officials *of the railway* are usually courteous. (Noun as Adjective.)
- (ii) The *chimney* smoke was the cause of complaint. (Preposition-Phrase.)
- (iii) That man *with a stop-watch* is a time-keeper. (Participle-Phrase.)
- (iv) The plan *prepared for an emergency* was put into operation. (Noun as Adjective.)
- (v) A *specially designed* theatre is to be built for the Festival. (Participle-Phrase.)

* * *

THE INFINITIVE as Adjective-Equivalent.

Examples:—

- (a) This is an occasion *to remember*.
- (b) I have nothing *to say*.
- (c) There is no need *to make such a noise*.

Here the Infinitive or Infinitive-Phrase qualifies the preceding Noun/Pronoun.

In (a) 'to remember' resembles 'memorable' (single Adjective).

In (b) 'to say' corresponds to 'for saying' (Preposition-Phrase equivalent to Adjective).

In (c) 'to make such a noise' corresponds to 'for such a noise' (Preposition-Phrase).

EXERCISE

Write sentences meaning much the same as the following, but using Infinitives as Adjective-Equivalents:—

    Example: There is one *additional* thing.
    There is one thing *to add*.

(i) Eventually he found an opportunity *for escaping*.
(ii) The question *under consideration* is whether you should resign.
(iii) The offence is not a *trivial* one.
(iv) The profit is not *negligible*.
(v) It was an *unforgettable* experience.

* * *

ADJECTIVE CLAUSES, as we shall see in more detail later (Chapter XVIII), are equivalent to Adjectives. One example will suffice here:—

Compare: The only explanation *that we could think of* was that the ship had sunk. (Adjective Clause.)
with: The only *possible* explanation was that the ship had sunk. (Adjective.)

EXERCISES

A. Analyse the following sentences and classify the Adjective-Equivalents under suitable headings:—

(i) A lady in a huge hat sat right in front of me.
(ii) The skater gave an exhibition to be marvelled at.

(iii) Swimming steadily, he crossed the Channel in record time.
(iv) John's present to me was a book token.
(v) Shelled and bombed continually, Dover suffered considerable damage.
(vi) A policeman with a truncheon gave the demonstrator chained to the railings something to think about.
(vii) The Army stores kept large stocks of canned meat.
(viii) A moving staircase is usually called an escalator.
(ix) His classroom behaviour was not an example to be imitated.
(x) Without looking round, he dropped a bundle of letters into the pillar-box at the end of the street.

B. Rewrite the following sentences using single Adjectives instead of the Adjective-Equivalents, and making any other alterations necessary:—

(i) He seemed lacking in resolution.
(ii) Give me something to eat.
(iii) A dog with an injured paw was trying to jump the gate.
(iv) This cheese is noted throughout the world.
(v) The decision was a Navy matter, not an Army one.
(vi) All the hotels in the neighbourhood were full.
(vii) His visit to Belgium was producing valuable results.
(viii) The experience was imprinted on his memory.
(ix) There were few candidates to choose from.
(x) He was a student of medicine.

CHAPTER XIII

ADVERB-EQUIVALENTS

Adverb-Equivalents fall into three classes:—

(*a*) The Infinitive.
(*b*) Preposition-Phrases.
(*c*) Adverb Clauses.

The INFINITIVE as Adverb-Equivalent. The Infinitive may be used Adverbially to qualify a Verb or an Adjective.

With a Verb it usually indicates:—

(*a*) Purpose. The plumber came *to mend* the broken pipe.
(*b*) Reason. I was surprised *to hear* him speak French.
(*c*) Result. I may not survive *to report* my experience.

With an Adjective it generally suggests:—

(*d*) Manner. The puzzle was hard *to solve*.

EXERCISES

A. Example: He ran *to catch* his train.
'to catch': Infinitive equivalent to Adverb of Purpose, extending Verb 'ran'.

Describe in a similar way the nature and function of the Infinitives in the following sentences:—

(i) Few people will live to see the end of all wars.
(ii) Most people eat to live, but some live to eat.
(iii) He was quick to appreciate the difficulties.
(iv) She set a trap to catch the mouse.
(v) We were relieved to find that they were ready to co-operate.

B. We have examined Infinitives as equivalents—

to Nouns: *To die* is but *to sleep*.
or Adjectives: He was a man *to be admired*.
or Adverbs: He stood up *to continue* his speech.

State the nature and function of the Infinitives in the following sentences:—

(i) The officer ordered his men to shoot.
(ii) He was disappointed to receive no reply.
(iii) His handwriting was hard to read.
(iv) Have you anything to declare?
(v) The safest measure was to take cover.
(vi) We stopped a moment to admire the landscape.
(vii) The film was called 'A Night to Remember'.
(viii) He made a last minute dash, to reach the barrier just in time.
(ix) To turn over a new leaf is easier said than done.
(x) The worst thing to do is to worry.

* * *

The PREPOSITION-PHRASE as Adverb-Equivalent.

The Preposition-Phrase is extremely common; it can perform many useful jobs. In addition to acting as Adjective-Equivalent (see page 72) it can act as Adverb-Equivalent.

The two patterns are quite different in function, though much the same in form:—

              Preposition-Phrase

NOUN   PREPOSITION + NOUN = ADJECTIVE
The man   with   the scar
was not seen   for   days
VERB   PREPOSITION + NOUN = ADVERB

              Preposition-Phrase

Whereas the Adjectival Preposition-Phrase is descriptive, its Adverbial counterpart adds to a Verb circumstances such as Time, Place and Manner.

The types of Adverbial Preposition-Phrase include:—

(a) Time: *In the morning* he telephoned again.
(b) Place: The meeting was held *near the church*.
(c) Manner: The speaker was greeted *with enthusiasm*.
(d) Degree: *To some extent* the result was anticipated.
(e) Reason: *For security reasons* he concealed his identity.
(f) Purpose: He went to the village hall *for a game of chess*.

Note.—In many Time-Phrases the Preposition is omitted, e.g.:—

    He stayed at home *every Sunday* (compare: *on Sunday*).

This ordinary Adverb classification does not cover two rather similar relationships, involving persons rather than things, which are best considered here: the 'to'-phrase and the 'by'-phrase.

We have already mentioned the 'to/for him' pattern in connection with the Indirect Object (see page 38).

Preposition-Phrases of this type, indicating the person interested in an action, do add meaning to the Verb, and can therefore be treated as Adverb-Equivalents. They often resemble Adverbs of Place: compare 'Bring it *to me*' with 'Bring it *here*'.

The distinction between this kind of phrase and the Indirect Object construction, though sometimes artificial, is worth preserving:—

The basis of: I offered him a cigarette is:—

   N/P   V   I.O. N/P   D.O. N/P
   I   — offered — him — cigarette

Compare: I offered a cigarette to him:—

   N/P   V   D.O. N.P.
   I   —   offered   —   cigarette
                   | |
               to him   a
               ADV   ADJ

Similarly, the Preposition-Phrase 'by . . .' denoting the agent or instrument of the action may conveniently be treated as the equivalent of an Adverb (often suggesting Manner):—

      He was killed *by gunmen*.
      He was killed *by a stray bullet*.

(Compare: He was killed *by mistake*.)

This construction obviously arises after a Verb in the Passive Voice, i.e. where the Subject is the receiver or sufferer of the action.

EXERCISE

Example: His remarks were received in complete silence.

'in complete silence': Adverbial Preposition-Phrase of Manner extending Verb 'were received'.

Describe the nature and function of the Adverbial Preposition-Phrases in the following sentences:—

(i) The horse bolted down the street.
(ii) He dropped into the club for a game of billiards.
(iii) His pleasure was to some extent spoilt by his friend's strange behaviour.
(iv) After the presentation he was introduced to the mayor.
(v) For the sake of peace he bought his son a rocking-horse.
(vi) His application was rejected without comment.
(vii) Next Wednesday evening I shall talk on butterflies.
(viii) The early morning train was delayed by fog.
(ix) He signalled to his sister to keep quiet.
(x) Every week without fail he played squash at the village hall.

* * *

ADVERB CLAUSES, as we shall see in more detail later (Chapter XIX), are equivalent to Adverbs. One example will suffice here:—

Compare: He fought *as if his life depended on it.* (Adverb Clause.)

with: He fought *desperately*. (Adverb.)

EXERCISES

A. Analyse the following sentences and classify the Adverb-Equivalents in as much detail as you can:—

  (i) After dinner he retired to the drawing-room to have a smoke.
  (ii) At the board meeting his offer was received in silence.
  (iii) He took off a slipper to throw at the cat.
  (iv) Their losses were in some measure reduced by the sale of equipment.
  (v) His explanation was difficult to follow.
  (vi) In order to make a good impression he put on his best uniform.
  (vii) Tell that to the marines.
  (viii) I was impressed by his skill.
  (ix) To save time, will you address all letters to my office?
  (x) For ten years he practised hard at the piano without success.

B. Substitute single Adverbs for the Adverb-Equivalents in the following, making any other alterations necessary:—

  (i) The results were on the whole favourable.
  (ii) The sentence was executed without delay.
  (iii) It was too hot to bear.
  (iv) To end up with, here is a piano duet.
  (v) He led the field from start to finish.

CHAPTER XIV

REVISION

For easy reference the main facts about ordinary Simple Sentences and Equivalents can be summarised as follows:—

A. A normal Simple Sentence contains items from the following:—

        Subject.
        Verb.
        Direct Object.
        Indirect Object.
        Subject Complement.
        Object Complement.

B. Its basic pattern will normally be one of the following:—

        $S + V$.
        $S + V + D.O.$
        $S + V + S.C.$
        $S + V + I.O. + D.O.$
        $S + V + D.O. + O.C.$

C. The Verb may be a single word, a Verb-Group (e.g. might have been swimming), or a Compound Verb (e.g. rubbed out).

D. A Subject and any Object will be a Noun or Noun-Equivalent; that is, one of the following:—

        Noun.
        Pronoun.
        Verb-Noun (Gerund or Infinitive).
        Adjective.
        Noun Clause.

E. A Complement will be

either: Noun or Noun-Equivalent as above,
or: Adjective or Adjective-Equivalent; that is, one of the following:—

Adjective.
Verb-Adjective (Present or Past Participle).
Preposition-Phrase.
Noun.
Infinitive.

(The Adjective Clause cannot be used as a Complement.)

F. Any of these basic items may have an extension.

G. The extension of a Noun or Noun-Equivalent will be an Adjective or Adjective-Equivalent (including the Adjective Clause).

H. The extension of a Verb or Adjective (or equivalent) will be an Adverb or Adverb-Equivalent; that is, one of the following:—

Adverb.
Infinitive.
Preposition-Phrase.
Adverb Clause.

REVISION EXERCISES

A. Reconstruct the Simple Sentences which produce the following analyses:—

(i)   N/P   V
      lifeboat   —   sank
         | |
      the water-   within a few
      logged/over-   minutes/like
      loaded with   a stone
      survivors
      ADJ   ADV

(ii) N/P   V   D.O. N/P.   O.C. ADJ
      lighting — made   — reading — difficult
         | | |
      the poor/in after   extremely
      the library dark
      ADJ   ADV   ADV

(iii) N/P   V   I.O. N/P.   D.O. N/P
      commander—gave   —   forces   —   orders
         | | | |
        the   thereupon   his re-   to restart
                              maining
      ADJ   ADV   ADJ   ADJ

(iv) N/P   V   S.C. N/P
      vessel   — became   —   wreck
         | | |
      the/heeling   soon   a total
      ADJ   ADV   ADJ

(v)   N/P   V   D.O. N/P
      boy   — made   —   fishing-rod
         | | |
      the/in the   with a long   a
      brown jersey branch
      ADJ   ADV   ADJ

B. Reconstruct Simple Sentences from the following information:—

BASIS	EXTENSIONS
(i) Subj: weather	the fine/unexpected at that time of the year
Verb: gave	the next day
I.O.: yachtsman	the impatient young
D.O.: opportunity	an/of sailing again
(ii) Subj: prefects	
Verb: may cane	in some schools/for certain offences
D.O.: boys	junior
(iii) Subj: Eric	young
Verb: ought to become	with practice/soon
S.C.: bowler	a useful spin
(iv) Subj: pole	the telegraph
Verb: crashed	without warning/ suddenly/across the road
(v) Subj: enthusiasm	an unbounded/for rock-climbing
Verb: made	
D.O.: boys	both the
O.C.: reckless	utterly

C. Pick out the Preposition-Phrases in the following. State whether they are equivalent to Adjectives or Adverbs and name the items they qualify:—

(i) The water near the old mill was very deep.
(ii) They used to swim near the old mill.
(iii) An exhibition of paintings by modern artists will be opened in the near future by the Lord Mayor.

(iv) To everybody's surprise the favourite horse dropped out at the first jump.

(v) No-one with any sense would walk right up to the edge of a precipice after dark without a light.

D. For the items printed in italics in the following sentences substitute equivalents of the kind indicated, making alterations in meaning and phrasing where necessary:—

Example: He always swam *early*. (Prep-Phrase = Adverb.)

He always swam *before breakfast*.

(i) He found himself *naked*. (Preposition-Phrase = Adjective.)

(ii) There is nothing better after exercise than *a cold plunge*. (Gerund = Noun.)

(iii) Her face, *red* with weeping, was a distressing sight. (Past Participle = Adjective.)

(iv) The leading lady suddenly *collapsed* on the stage. (Compound Verb = Verb.)

(v) A tall negro was the *leader* in the race. (Adjective = Noun.)

(vi) She complained that she had no dress *suitable* for the ball. (Infinitive = Adjective.)

(vii) The aeroplane flew *seawards*. (Preposition-Phrase = Adverb.)

(viii) *Ignorance* is not always a disgrace. (Infinitive = Noun.)

(ix) He was found *full-length* on the ground. (Present Participle = Adjective.)

(x) Lighthouses need to be built *durably*. (Infinitive = Adverb.)

E. Analyse:

  (i) The house with the red roof was struck by lightning some years ago.
  (ii) Will you ask the headmaster to let me go?
  (iii) His head heavily bandaged, he reported to the reception centre.
  (iv) Stop shouting so loudly.
  (v) Without further delay we pulled up the ladder.
  (vi) The magistrate disapproved most strongly of the drunk and disorderly.
  (vii) The young man in plus fours put his golf clubs on the luggage rack.
  (viii) To relax in vigilance gives the enemy the opportunity for a surprise attack.
  (ix) You will find my boots on the top shelf in the cupboard next to the fireplace in the kitchen.
  (x) Frequent stopping and starting made the engine too hot to touch.

PART THREE
ASSEMBLING THE ITEMS

CHAPTER XV
PROXIMITY

Examine these sentences :—

(*a*) Only he asked to be excused from morning school on Tuesdays.

(*b*) He only asked to be excused from morning school on Tuesdays.

(*c*) He asked only to be excused from morning school on Tuesdays.

(*d*) He asked to be excused only from morning school on Tuesdays.

(*e*) He asked to be excused from morning school on Tuesdays only.

These five sentences all contain exactly the same words. But they have quite different meanings. This variation depends entirely on a variation in the order of the items. The word 'only' attaches itself to (i.e. extends) an item next to it, usually the one following :—

(*a*) Who asked?
 Only he asked.
(*b*) What did he say?
 He *only asked* to be excused . . .
(*c*) What did he ask for?
 He asked *only to be excused* from morning school . . .

(*d*) From what did he ask to be excused?
He asked to be excused *only from morning school* . . .
(*e*) For what days did he ask to be excused?
He asked to be excused . . . on *Tuesdays only*.

Obviously, to convey an exact meaning, you must be careful to keep together items which are thought of together. Extensions, for instance, should be as near as possible to the items they extend. This is the RULE of PROXIMITY.

Analysis often makes clear, not only a breaking of this rule, but also the necessary correction, e.g.:—

WRONG: Every town *almost* has its own library.

N/P	V	D.O. N/P
town	— has —	library
|	|	|
every ←	(almost)	its own
ADJ	ADV	ADJ

RIGHT: *Almost* every town has its own library.

EXERCISES

A. The Rule of Proximity has been broken in the following sentences. Make the necessary corrrection and explain it:—

(i) Snow only falls in winter.
(ii) He accepted the offer made to him gladly.
(iii) The conductor of the tram escaped injury alone.
(iv) He had breakfast in bed usually on Sundays.
(v) (Sydney has a good harbour.) Harwich has also a natural harbour.

B. Example: *Unhappily* he lived alone.
He lived alone *unhappily*.

Change the meaning of the following sentences by moving the words in italics:—

(i) I *once* played hockey for the school.
(ii) He denied that he had answered the call *promptly*.
(iii) He hoped to be able to play cricket *often*.
(iv) The doctor *again* asked the patient to put out his tongue.
(v) You may *well* doubt whether he will play.

* * *

The misplacement of single words is less usual and probably less serious than the wrong positioning of phrases. A misplaced phrase is often misleading and sometimes absurd:—

(a) The judge asked the witness to speak up several times.
(b) Rifles were dropped from aeroplanes attached to parachutes.
(c) Hurrying along the street a banana-skin escaped his notice.

Note.—The incorrect use of the Participial Phrase as in (b) and (c)—not attached to its proper 'subject'—is so common that it has a name of its own, the UNRELATED PARTICIPLE.

EXERCISES

A. Correct the above sentences and those below by applying the Rule of Proximity:—

(i) Macbeth was returning home after the battle with his brother-officer Banquo.

(ii) A woman was leading a Pekinese dog wearing high-heeled shoes.
(iii) They tried to find it without success.
(iv) Micah joined the Duke of Monmouth with his friends Reuben and Decimus.
(v) Sheep-dogs need careful training by their owners while still puppies.
(vi) Marah had imprisoned the two coastguards whom Jim had seen the day before on the cliff-top in the cave.
(vii) Standing close behind the stumps, the ball hit the wicket-keeper in the mouth.
(viii) One day along came a piper with a pipe of smooth straight cane, dressed in red and yellow.
(ix) I found the boots I wear for gardening in the bathroom.
(x) (Mr. Polly chose to die on the Sabbath.) Hence it was on a Sunday evening that he planned to commit suicide.

B. Make two quite different sentences by putting the given phrase in two different places in the sentence:—

(i) before February 3rd
please let me know whether you are coming.
(ii) by Shaw
a volume of plays lay on the bed.
(iii) without delay
he applied for permission to open a shop.
(iv) peering over the edge of the cliff
the policeman saw a suspicious-looking person.
(v) unnoticed by the others
he found footprints in the mud.

CHAPTER XVI

LINK-WORDS

We have seen that even a Simple Sentence may contain a large number of items. Attached to a basis of up to four items may be as many extensions as sense will allow.

The reader must be able immediately to grasp the connection between the various items. He is helped in this, as we have already noticed, by:—

(*a*) Pattern. We take for granted such familiar orders as Subject-Verb-Object, for instance.

(*b*) Proximity. Items connected in thought are close together in wording.

(*c*) Prepositions. These indicate the relationship between the Noun/Pronoun they govern and some other item.

Even in Simple Sentences these three factors are often not enough to cope with the large number of items and relationships. In non-Simple (Compound and Complex) Sentences their limitations are still more obvious. To supplement them we use a variety of words (mostly short ones) which we may call LINKS or COUPLINGS. Several Parts of Speech are concerned.

If we anticipate Chapter XVII by accepting a Compound Sentence as one containing two or more equal Predications, and a Complex Sentence as one containing one or more Predications subordinate to the main Predication, we can classify Links as:—

(i) Co-ordinating—joining equal items,
and (ii) Sub-ordinating—joining unequal items.

In more detail, the possibilities are:—

```
                            LINKS
                    Co-ordinating   Subordinating
          ⎧ Simple    Conjunction   Preposition
          ⎪ Compound  Conjunction       —
Sentence ⎨                         ⎧ Relative
          ⎪                        ⎪   Pronoun
          ⎩ Complex       —        ⎨ Relative
                                   ⎪   Adverb
                                   ⎩ Conjunction
```

The CO-ORDINATING CONJUNCTION joins two or more *equal* items—two or more equal words, phrases, or (in Compound Sentences) predications, e.g.:—

(*a*) Tom *and* his cousin were sworn enemies.
(*b*) He worked slowly *but* methodically.
(*c*) Slugs are *neither* useful *nor* ornamental.
(*d*) *Whether* working *or* playing he was always cheerful.
(*e*) He worked hard, *yet* he never seemed tired.

The SUBORDINATING link includes:—

A. Within a Simple Sentence or other single predication, the Preposition (see page 71):—

That man *with* a monocle is a police agent.
Notice in particular the use of the Preposition with the Gerund:—

While waiting for the train, he read a newspaper.

B. In a Complex sentence, RELATIVE PRONOUNS, RELATIVE ADVERBS, and SUBORDINATING CONJUNCTIONS. The Relative Pronouns 'who', 'which', and 'that', and the Relative Adverbs 'where' and 'when' are sometimes used in a Continuative sense, with very little, if any, suggestion of subordination:—

> I met Mr. Higgins, *who* seemed very pleased to see me (who = and he).
> John brought his aeroplane, *which* amused us for hours (which = and it).
> We took it into the shed, *where* we pulled it to pieces (where = and there).
> This occupied us until tea-time, *when* we remembered the rehearsal (when = and then).

It is in fact possible to treat sentences such as these as Compound Sentences, with *Co*-ordinate clauses.

But these same links are used as well for true subordination, as are also Subordinating Conjunctions such as:—

> before, after, while, until, since, although, because, unless, so that, in case, as, if.

The main relationships indicated are: Time, Place, Manner, Cause, Purpose, Result, Condition, Concession. (See Chapter XIX on Adverb Clauses.)

You may have noticed that certain Links (e.g. while) appear both as Prepositions and as Subordinating Conjunctions. The difference is that the Preposition governs a phrase, whereas the Conjunction introduces a Clause (i.e. a Predication with its own Finite Verb). Hence:—

> *Before* entering the house he prowled round the garden (before = Preposition).
> *Before* he entered the house, he prowled round the garden (before = Conjunction).

This difference is slight, but it reveals a difference of emphasis. The Preposition-Phrase attracts rather less attention than the Clause. (See also Chapter XXVII.)

EXERCISES

A. Pick out the link-words in the following and classify them under the headings: Preposition, Relative Pronoun, Relative Adverb, Co-ordinating Conjunction, Subordinating Conjunction:—

There were three candidates in each ward for the council seats which were vacant. As the time of the election drew near, excitement ran high throughout the town and a record poll was expected. The schools, church halls and other places where voting was to take place were prepared for a busy day. In due course canvassing stopped and the polling booths were opened, but the rush was much less than had been expected.

B. Insert suitable link-words in the following:—

(i) He pressed his foot on the self-starter . . . nothing happened.

(ii) The result was far different . . . what he had expected.

(iii) He refused to accept the job . . . he was granted a fortnight's holiday a year.

(iv) He has always been . . . punctual in attendance . . . I think he must . . . be ill . . . away from home.

(v) . . . he scored very high marks, he was not awarded a scholarship.

LINK-WORDS

C. Improve the following sentences by substituting better link-words for those in italics (and making any other adjustments consequently necessary):—

(i) In the cave he found an old chest, *also* a compass.

(ii) I asked the way of a policeman *and* he gave me detailed directions.

(iii) He could not see over the heads of the people in front, *so* he climbed a lamp-post.

(iv) *When* he was in the cellar, someone knocked at the front door.

(v) *When* we were approaching the village, we heard the sound of a fair.

PART FOUR

MULTIPLE SENTENCES

CHAPTER XVII

COMPOUND SENTENCES

Taking the term 'Multiple' to mean 'Containing more than one Clause' (i.e. Predication), we shall distinguish between three kinds of MULTIPLE SENTENCE, according to the numbers of Main Clauses and Dependent or Subordinate Clauses (i.e. clauses grammatically less important than Main Clauses) which each type contains.

	Main	Dependent
(a) Compound Sentence	2+	0
(b) Complex Sentence	1	1+
(c) Compound-Complex Sentence	2+	1+

(2+ = two or more)

A Simple Sentence contains only one Predication. A COMPOUND SENTENCE contains two or more similar Predications:—

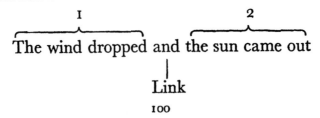

Note.—(*a*) Each Predication could have been a Simple Sentence.

(*b*) Each Predication contains its own Finite Verb.

(*c*) The Predications are linked by a Co-ordinating Conjunction ('and').

(*d*) Predications in these circumstances are more usually known as Clauses.

(*e*) The Compound Sentence may contain two or more Clauses.

Where a Compound Sentence contains a series of Clauses, more often than not only the last two are coupled together by a Conjunction:—

> The lights were dimmed, the music stopped, the curtain rose, *and* the play began.

Sometimes the couplings are omitted altogether, only the punctuation showing that the items are not separate Simple Sentences:—

> I came, I saw, I conquered.

Where a series of Clauses in a Compound Sentence has a common subject, that subject is often stated in the first Predication only:—

> *He* pushed, pulled, wrenched and twisted the handle, but failed to open the door.

Compound Sentences could be analysed as series of Predications:—

The tall man darted on to the platform, but just missed the departing train.

```
        N/P           V
        man    —    darted
         |            |
       the tall    on to the
                   platform
        ADJ          ADV
but
        N/P           V            D.O. N/P
        (he)   —    missed   —     train
                      |              |
                     just       the departing
                     ADV            ADJ
```

But this is unnecessarily detailed and long. It will usually be sufficient to split the Sentence into its Clauses and show the connection between them.

The Clauses of a Compound Sentence are known as 'Main' Clauses; the grammatical term for 'equal' is 'co-ordinate'.

Hence:—

(a) *Main Clause*   The tall man darted on to the platform

(b) *Main Clause co-ordinate with* (a)   but just missed the train.

EXERCISE

Analyse the following sentences similarly to the above:—

(i) The young urchin picked up a brick and hurled it through the window.

(ii) He argued, stormed and even begged, yet he failed to win his case.
(iii) Either you must pay your subscription or you must resign from the society.
(iv) She neither spoke nor made any sign.
(v) Pick up your case, walk to the end of the street, and wait there, but do not on any account turn round.

CHAPTER XVIII

COMPLEX SENTENCES: ADJECTIVE CLAUSES

Three young journalists reported a boxing contest in which, as Journalist No. 1 wrote:—

> The Bermondsey Bombshell received a blow on the chin. It sent him reeling across the ring.

This pattern of two short Simple Sentences gave him the short, staccato effect he wanted.

But Journalist No. 2 wanted to save his staccato effects for a later climax. For the earlier, lesser moment he found one Simple Sentence, with a Participial Phrase, sufficient:—

> The Bermondsey Bombshell, receiving a blow on the chin, reeled across the ring.

Journalist No. 3 thought both statements important enough for Clauses, but not for whole Sentences. So he wrote a Compound Sentence:—

> The Bermondsey Bombshell received a blow on the chin and reeled across the ring.

The sub-editors of the three newspapers 'blue-pencilled' each effort, and substituted:—

> The Bermondsey Bombshell received a blow on the chin which sent him reeling across the ring.

ADJECTIVE CLAUSES

This neater, more compact wording could be analysed as if it were a single Simple Sentence:—

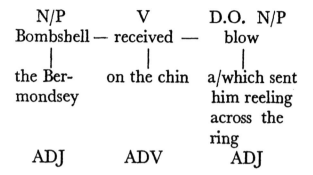

But the word-cluster 'which sent him reeling across the ring' is itself a Predication or Clause, based on the Finite Verb 'sent'. It is in fact an ADJECTIVE CLAUSE extending the Noun 'blow'.

The two Predications may therefore be set out as:—

(a) *Main Clause*   The Bermondsey Bombshell received a blow on the chin
(b) *Adjective Clause extending 'blow'*   which sent him reeling across the ring.

This kind of Sentence, containing one Main and one or more Dependent or Subordinate Clauses, is called COMPLEX.

The Main Clause corresponds to a Simple Sentence.

The Adjective Clause has a Finite Verb ('sent'), but it cannot get along on its own; it depends on the Main Clause, to which it is coupled by the link-word 'which'.

Link-words like 'which', 'who' and 'that' (when 'that' is equivalent to 'which') are not Conjunctions but RELATIVE PRONOUNS, i.e. Pronouns which 'relate' to a preceding Noun/Pronoun (sometimes called the ANTECEDENT).

One Complex Sentence may contain several Adjective Clauses, each extending a previously mentioned Noun/Pronoun:—

> This is the malt that lay in the house that Jack built.

The Relative Pronoun (especially 'that') is often understood rather than stated:—

> That is the kind of bicycle (that) I want.

EXERCISES

A. Analyse the following on the model given above:—

- (i) Tennis is the game I like best of all.
- (ii) The game that I like best of all is tennis.
- (iii) The leading actor, about whom I had heard so much, gave a very poor performance.
- (iv) The book from which the Prime Minister quoted in the speech he made to the House of Commons was by a young soldier who had been killed in action.
- (v) One thing he could not do was to send for the police.

B. Rewrite the following as Complex Sentences, containing Main and Adjective Clauses:—

- (i) He dropped the lamp and it caught the curtains alight.
- (ii) The floor was made of wood and this had gone rotten.
- (iii) I reported the discovery to the police, and they sent along a C.I.D. man.

(iv) Here is the register; we have signed our names in it.
(v) That is the man; I wrote to you about him last week.

C. Rewrite the following, substituting Adjective Clauses for the Participial Phrases:—

(i) The fugitive, not having had a meal for days, was found in a state of exhaustion.
(ii) The curtains, drawn as a protection against the mid-day sun, were later pulled back.
(iii) The old man, smoking his pipe and reading the newspaper, seemed quite content.
(iv) Beaten to the ground by the heavy rain, the corn yielded a poor harvest.
(v) Being over six feet tall, the officer was able to rescue the kitten stranded on the narrow ledge.

D. Notice the difference in meaning between:—

(a) The books, which were in poor condition, were scrapped ; and
(b) The books which were in poor condition were scrapped.

Pick out the Adjective Clauses in the following and state whether they are descriptive (like (a)) or restrictive (like (b)):—

(i) This is the house that Jack built.
(ii) Its garden, which is extensive, has not been dug for years.
(iii) My uncle, for whom I have considerable regard, is a teetotaller.
(iv) The master interviewed those boys who were in their last year at school.
(v) The flowers he grew were all annuals.

Before which of these two types of Adjective Clause do you sometimes find 'that'?

Before which type is the Relative Pronoun sometimes left out altogether?

* * *

The Rule of PROXIMITY—that an extension must be close to the item it extends—applies very strongly to Adjective Clauses. The Antecedent is often one of several Nouns or Pronouns in the sentence. But the reader should not have to pause to make sure which of them is really the Antecedent.

An extreme example of the fault is:—

> A tin can struck him on the head, which was fortunately empty.

Here the Relative Pronoun 'which' and its Adjective Clause seem for one absurd moment to apply to 'head'. A regrouping is necessary to bring the Adjective Clause next to its proper Antecedent 'tin can':—

> A tin can, which was fortunately empty, struck him on the head.

EXERCISE

Correct the following Sentences by moving the Adjective Clauses nearer to their proper Antecedents:—

> (i) There is an old barometer on the wall which is nearly a hundred years old.
> (ii) He had a sabre-cut across one cheek which showed up white and livid.

(iii) I had four pieces of plaster on my face, which I had accumulated by many falls.
(iv) There are two big gates at the bottom of the drive, which are falling to pieces.
(v) The floors are littered with debris which creak when you tread on them.
(vi) The stonepit was near the village of Raveloe, which resembled an abandoned quarry.
(vii) Fire extinguishers put out the fire by spreading a blanket of carbon dioxide over it which excludes oxygen.
(viii) Mr. Brown at last mounted his horse, who was wearing leather knee-breeches.
(ix) The boy was hiding behind his class-mates for whom the master was looking.
(x) The old house had no bathroom in which I was born.

CHAPTER XIX

COMPLEX SENTENCES: ADVERB CLAUSES

Whereas Nouns and Pronouns have Adjective extensions, Verbs and Adjectives have Adverb extensions.

Since any Extension may be word, phrase or clause, we may expect to find, in addition to Adjective Clauses extending Nouns or Pronouns, ADVERB CLAUSES extending Verbs or Adjectives, answering such questions as 'where? when? why? how?' about the Verb, or 'how (much)?' about the Adjective.

Examples:—

(a) As he approached the house, the front door opened.

| *Main Clause* | The front door opened |
| *Adverb Clause of Time extending 'opened'* | As he approached the house. |

(b) The hill was so steep that he had to dismount.

| *Main Clause* | The hill was so steep |
| *Adverb Clause of Degree extending 'steep'* | that he had to dismount. |

These are Complex Sentences, the Dependent or Subordinate Clause being Adverbial instead of Adjectival and linked to a Verb or Adjective instead of to a Noun or Pronoun.

The link-word introducing the Adverb Clause is one of a variety of Conjunctions indicating more or less the kind of connection between the two Clauses joined.

The following table is a rough guide to the main possibilities:—

Type	Answering	Characteristic Conjunctions
1. Manner	How?	as
2. Time	When?	when, till, while, before, after, since
3. Place	Where?	where, whence, whither
4. Cause, Reason	Why?	as, because, since
5. Condition	On what condition?	if, unless, whether
6. Purpose	For what purpose?	(so) that, lest
7. Result	With what result?	that
8. Degree, Comparison	How? How much?	as, than
9. Concession	In spite of what?	though, although

Notes.—(a) This table is only a rough guide. The Conjunction may give a hint, but the decisive factor is the nature of the work done by the Adverb Clause.

(b) Adverb Clauses may extend, not only Verbs and Adjectives, but also Adverbs, i.e. they may extend extensions as well as basic items, e.g.:—

> The man was so badly injured that he died within a few minutes.

Here the Adverb Clause 'that . . . minutes' is one of Result (or possibly Degree) extending the Adverb 'badly'.

EXERCISES

A. Analyse the following into Main and Adverb Clauses:—

    (i) Though he practised regularly at the piano, he made no progress.
    (ii) I shall be there whether you come or not.
    (iii) Nothing has been heard of Tom since he sailed for India.
    (iv) Since you ignore my advice, I shall not again offer to help you.
    (v) He was more worried about it than he cared to admit.
    (vi) He was breathing as if he had been running hard.
    (vii) If the drought continues much longer, water will be so scarce that it will have to be rationed.
    (viii) Because the tides were unusually high, the boys could not leave the boat where it normally stayed.
    (ix) While the air-raid was in progress, the people behaved as calmly as they had during practice raids.
    (x) Although he was on holiday he set the alarm-clock, so that he would be awakened at six o'clock.

B. Analyse the following sentences, which may contain Adjective and/or Adverb Clauses:—

    (i) He was concerned lest the news should come during his absence.

ADVERB CLAUSES

(ii) Until I find a more suitable house, I shall remain where I am.

(iii) The house where I now live has been so damaged that it is hardly habitable.

(iv) The policeman of whom I asked the way looked at me as if I were mad.

(v) If you collect all the papers and bring them along to me tomorrow, we can discuss the proposal Mr. Rigden has made before we decide on a definite answer.

(vi) The car we have hired this year is much older than the one we had last year.

(vii) After the earthquake, which destroyed the centre of the town, many buildings which were considered unsafe were pulled down.

(viii) Whilst those who had lost their homes were wandering aimlessly, those who had survived unhurt were thanking Providence for their escape.

(ix) This is the cat that chased the rat that ate the malt that lay in the house that Jack built.

(x) Wherever you go, I shall follow.

C. Rewrite the following groups of sentences as single sentences, using somewhere the types of Clause indicated in brackets:—

(i) It was raining steadily half an hour before the time for the game to begin.
The cricket match was not cancelled.
(Adverb Clause of Concession.)

(ii) A film is being shown at the Granada.
This film is a Laurel and Hardy comedy.
(Adjective Clause.)

(iii) The two young men turned down a dark side street.
We were following them.
They seemed afraid of being followed.
(Adjective Clause; Adverb Clause of Manner.)

(iv) The guy-ropes were very slack.
The tent seemed likely to collapse.
The tent had already given us a lot of trouble.
(Adverb Clause of Result; Adjective Clause.)

(v) The building was being demolished.
There was danger of falling masonry.
Traffic was diverted.
(Two Adverb Clauses of Time.)

CHAPTER XX

COMPLEX SENTENCES: NOUN CLAUSES

The two types of Complex Sentence we have so far studied can be tabulated:—

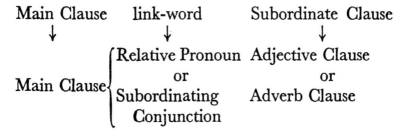

Adjective and Adverb Clauses act as Extensions, of Nouns/Pronouns and Verbs/Adjectives/Adverbs respectively. But there is a third type of Subordinate Clause—the NOUN CLAUSE—which commonly belongs to the Basis of the sentence. Doing the work of a Noun, it can be, for instance, Subject, Object (Direct or Indirect) or Complement of a Verb. In such cases the Main Clause, since it lacks part of the basis, often makes little or no sense on its own.

The Noun Clause can also operate like a Noun in an extension. A Preposition-Phrase, for example, may consist of Preposition and Noun Clause, in which case the Clause is said to be the Object of the Preposition.

And lastly, the Noun Clause can stand alongside—i.e. in Apposition to—a Noun or Pronoun.

Examples will make these various uses clear:—

1. Noun Clause as Subject of a Verb.
What fortune-tellers prophesy does not always come true.

Compare the Noun-Phrase in:—

The prophecies of fortune-tellers do not . . .
The analysis is:—

(a) *Main Clause*   does not always come true.
(b) *Noun Clause*   what fortune-tellers prophesy.
  Subject of 'does not come'.

2. Noun Clause as Object of a Verb.

(i) Direct Object.
   We heard *that John had been promoted.*
Compare: We heard-of *John's promotion.*
(ii) Indirect Object.
   I shall give *whoever finds it* a reward.
Compare: I shall give *the finder* a reward.

3. Noun Clause as Complement of a Verb.

 (i) Subject-Complement.
  The question at issue was *whether he should resign or not.*
Compare: The question at issue was *his resignation.*
(ii) Object-Complement.
   Constant effort had made him *what he was.*
Compare: Constant effort had made him *like that.*

4. Noun Clause as Object of a Preposition.

   There is no objection to *what you propose.*
Compare: There is no objection to *your proposal.*

5. Noun Clause in Apposition to a Noun/Pronoun.
Two items in Apposition are interchangeable:—

   Mr. Baldwin, *the Prime Minister*, has resigned.

'The Prime Minister' is in Apposition to 'Mr. Baldwin', combining the two alternatives:—

Mr. Baldwin has resigned.
The Prime Minister has resigned.

Similarly the Noun Clause can take the place of a Noun to which it is in Apposition, as in:—

(i) The doubt *whether the match could be finished* was soon settled.
> (Noun Clause in Apposition to the Subject-Noun 'doubt'.)

(ii) The weather settled the question *whether the match* could be finished.
> (Noun Clause in Apposition to the Object-Noun 'question'.)

EXERCISES

A. Analyse the following sentences, which contain Main and Noun Clauses:—

(i) Nobody noticed that the prisoner had slipped away.
(ii) He resold his motor-cycle for what he had paid for it.
(iii) The cave was just what we were looking for.
(iv) What upset him was the feeling that he was suspected of dishonesty.
(v) He made the mistake of confusing what was customary with what was legal.
(vi) That money is the root of all evil is an arguable observation.
(vii) Constant over-eating had made him what his doctor had forecast.
(viii) That is what I want.
(ix) Nobody dared call the old man what we all thought him.

(x) The news that reinforcements were on the way reassured him that the garrison would not starve.

B. Analyse the following sentences, which contain Clauses of various kinds:—

(i) The cross-country runner, whose muddy appearance showed that the course was hard going, staggered up to the finishing-tape.
(ii) That the situation was grave became evident when the fleet, which had only just sailed for its autumn exercises, was suddenly recalled.
(iii) So that there should be no misunderstanding, he wrote down what he thought they ought to do.
(iv) I shall have nothing to do with what you propose unless you explain your scheme thoroughly and give me time to consider it.
(v) The next speaker, to whom everybody listened attentively, directed attention to the problem how they should collect arrears of subscriptions.
(vi) If I am given what I require, I will guarantee that those of you who are sensible will come to no harm.
(vii) Though you have been pressed for time, your work is just what I hoped for.
(viii) Where we camped was delightful.
(ix) As soon as they moved in, our new neighbours renamed their house what we feared—'Sea View'.
(x) The announcement that was made suggested that everybody should be indoors by ten o'clock, unless they had special permission.

COMPOUND-COMPLEX SENTENCES

We have so far dealt with three kinds of sentence:—

Type	No. of Clauses	
	Main	Sub
A. Simple	1	0
B. Compound	2+	0
C. Complex	1	1+

The fourth type is a combination of B and C:—

D. Compound-Complex	2+	1+

It has the two or more Main Clauses which make up a Compound Sentence, together with at least one Subordinate Clause.

EXERCISE

Analyse the following Compound-Complex Sentences:—

(i) While the batsmen were hesitating, cover-point fielded the ball and returned it smartly to the wicket-keeper.

(ii) The flowers which I had sown in the spring had grown well, but those I had planted out the previous autumn were a complete failure.

(iii) The sun was shining, the sea was calm, the beach was crowded, and the deck-chair attendants were busier than they had been for weeks.

(iv) Either we must do the journey in two stages or we must book berths in a sleeper which goes straight through.
(v) Wounded in both legs and suffering severely from shock and exposure, he collapsed and died soon after he was rescued.
(vi) He admitted that he had known the dead man but denied that he had murdered him.
(vii) The man was lying in what appeared a pool of blood, but no-one moved to help him.
(viii) The long days which he had spent sailing were what he missed most, but in time he became as contented as he had ever been.
(ix) As he felt tired, he sat down, picked up the newspaper and settled down to a restful afternoon.
(x) That he should pay Income Tax at all annoyed him very much, but that he should have to pay so much infuriated him.

CHAPTER XXII

REVISION

REVISION OF CLAUSE ANALYSIS

When you have extracted from a Sentence the first Main Clause, each of the remaining Clauses will fall under one of these headings:—

MAIN	co-ordinate with		(*a*), (*b*), etc.
ADJECTIVE	extending		N/P
ADVERB of	{ MANNER, TIME, PLACE, CAUSE, CONDITION, PURPOSE, RESULT, DEGREE, CONCESSION }	extending	V/ADJ/ADV
NOUN	{ SUBJECT of		V
	OBJECT of		V
	COMPLEMENT of		V
	OBJECT of		PREPOSITION
	in APPOSITION to }		N/P

REVISION EXERCISES

A. Classify the following sentences as Simple, Compound, Complex or Compound-Complex:—

(i) He seized the bat I was holding and ran off with it.

(ii) What amazed him was the speed of the train and its smooth running.
(iii) He sat back, delighted to be in England again and thoroughly enjoying his first sight for many years of the Kentish countryside.
(iv) Stop, look, and listen.
(v) No man I know has visited that mysterious place and returned alive.

B. What is wrong with the following sentences:—

(i) This king, if he caught anybody doing wrong, they were committed to trial in the arena.
(ii) The swirling oily water through which little light passes.
(iii) There was a crackling roar as the fire swept down on us, driven by a stiff breeze, and a pungent smell of smoke.
(iv) Gulliver heard a hammering, when he looked up he saw a wooden platform being erected.
(v) The firemen played water on the burning house, after the flames had subsided the policeman entered the building.

C. Describe the weakness in style of the following in grammatical terms. Improve them:—

(i) No one guessed that the real culprit was Dunstan Cass, the black sheep of Squire Cass's family, who had stolen the gold so that his brother Godfrey could pay back to his father some money which he had stolen from him for Dunstan, who was blackmailing him because of his secret marriage.

(ii) The officers return to kill Dimitri, but they find the doctor examining him and the doctor says that he has not more than ten days to live.

(iii) When the play was nearly over he came out of the theatre when the last scene began.

(iv) If the weather continues fine and if we wake up early enough, we could have a quiet swim before breakfast, if the tide is in.

(v) John notices that the room was empty and that the window was wide open, and he looked round quickly before the others arrived, but he did not find any clues and he began to wonder if he had been mistaken.

PART FIVE

PARAGRAPH PATTERNS

CHAPTER XXIII

INTRODUCTION: VARIETY V. REPETITION

Language is a live thing and it is risky to cut it up as if it were dead meat. We have already taken the risk of cutting up sentences to see how they work. We must now take the risk of cutting up whole paragraphs. Remembering that all definitions, analyses and classifications are artificial and that exceptions are countless, let us see how sentences work in the mass.

Sentences are made up of word-clusters which may be classified in a rough and ready way:—

(*a*) MC.   Main Clause.
(*b*) SBC.   Subordinate Clause.
(*c*) PHR.   Phrase, Verbal (with Participle, Gerund or Infinitive),
            or Non-Verbal (with Preposition).

In practice it is often impossible definitely to decide whether a given group of words is a separate word-cluster or part of a larger unit. But difference of opinion over such details is not likely to affect our main conclusions.

Examination of specimen passages will show a large variety of ways of assembling word-clusters into sentences. In particular there can be a wide variation of:—

    (*a*) The number of clusters.
    (*b*) The kind of clusters.
    (*c*) The order of clusters.

This variety can be—and most commonly is—used to avoid monotony. On the other hand, it is sometimes effective deliberately to shun variety and to repeat one pattern.

We shall examine Variety and Repetition in relation to the number, to the kind and to the order of word-clusters.

CHAPTER XXIV

NUMBER OF WORD-CLUSTERS

Here is a passage from a short story by a modern writer:—

Passage A

A door clicked. A step sounded. Someone came downstairs. The old man rolled from side to side, slobbering and dribbling. He had the appearance of one very drunk. Round the half-shut door slid a large, stooping Chinky, flashily dressed in East End ready-mades. Under the yellow skin was a slow flush. His eyes sparkled. His thin, black hair was disordered.

He moved towards Perce. Three coins jingled from his hand to the stretched hand of Perce. Old Joe wobbled. He saw them; they were gold.

Analysing the thirteen sentences in this passage into numbered clusters:—

	Sentence No.	Cluster No.
A door clicked.	1 MC	1
A step sounded.	2 MC	2
Someone came downstairs.	3 MC	3
The old man rolled from side to side, slobbering and dribbling.	4 MC+PHR	4, 5
He had the appearance of one very drunk.	5 MC	6

	Sentence No.	Cluster No.
Round the half-shut door slid a large, stooping Chinky, flashily dressed in East End ready-mades.	6PHR+MC+PHR	7, 8, 9
Under the yellow skin was a slow flush.	7 MC	10
His eyes sparkled.	8 MC	11
His thin, black hair was disordered.	9 MC	12
He moved towards Perce.	10 MC	13
Three coins jingled from his hand to the outstretched hand of Perce.	11 MC+PHR	14, 15
Old Joe wobbled.	12 MC	16
He saw them; they were gold.	13 MC+MC	17, 18

Here thirteen sentences yield some eighteen word-clusters. The writer has deliberately used many one-cluster sentences, to produce a jerky, dramatic effect.

Contrast this with the ratio of clusters to sentences in the opening paragraphs of Dr. Johnson's *Journey to the Western Islands*, which may be analysed as follows:—

Passage B

Sentence No.

1. I had desired to visit the Hebrides, or Western Isles of Scotland, so long (Cluster No. 1-MC) that I scarcely remember (2-SBC) how the wish was originally excited (3-SBC); and was in the autumn of 1773 induced to undertake the journey (4 and 5-MC

and PHR), by finding in Mr. Boswell a companion (6-PHR), whose acuteness would help my inquiry (7-SBC), and whose gaiety of conversation and civility of manners are sufficient to counteract the inconveniences of travel (8-SBC), in countries less hospitable (9-PHR) than we have passed (10-SBC).

2. On the eighteenth of August (11-PHR) we left Edinburgh (12-MC), a city too well known to admit description (13-PHR), and directed our course northward (14-MC), along the eastern coast of Scotland (15-PHR), accompanied the first day by another gentleman (16-PHR), who could stay with us only long enough to show us (17-SBC) how much we lost at separation (18-SBC).

Here the same number of word-clusters—eighteen—are grouped in only two sentences. Dr. Johnson uses the long, leisurely Compound-Complex sentences fashionable in his less hurried days.

But these two passages are extremes. We shall find something nearer the average in Winston Churchill's War Memoirs:—

Passage C

Sentence No.	Clusters Nos.	Kind
1. On June 13 I made my last visit to France for four years almost to a day.	1-3	PHR+MC+PHR
2. The French Government had now withdrawn to Tours, and tension had mounted steadily.	4-5	MC+MC

Sentence No.	Clusters Nos.	Kind
3. I took Edward Halifax and General Ismay with me, and Max Beaverbrook volunteered to come too.	6-7	MC+MC
4. In trouble he is always buoyant.	8	MC
5. This time the weather was cloudless, and we sailed over in the midst of our Hurricane squadron, making however a rather wider sweep to the southward than before.	9-12	MC+MC+ PHR
6. Arrived at Tours, we found the airport had been heavily bombed the night before, but we and all our escort landed smoothly in spite of the craters.	13-17	PHR+MC+ SBC+MC+ PHR

For ordinary purposes a ratio such as this—17 word-clusters in 6 sentences—is more satisfactory than either the high proportion of Simple Sentences in the first extract or the few extremely long sentences of the second.

The short sentence style is effective for dramatic story-telling. The long sentence, though out of date as used by Dr. Johnson, still has its uses—for presenting arguments or setting out historical facts, for instance:—

Passage D

But the worst period for sanitary conditions in the industrial regions was the middle of the Nineteenth Century rather than the beginning, because so many of the new houses had then had time to become slums, since no one repaired or drained them as the years went by.

The factory hands, like the miners, were brought together as a mass of employees face to face with an employer, who lived apart from them in a house of his own in a separate social atmosphere; whereas under the old rural system they had been scattered about—one, two or at most half a dozen hands to each farm—in close and therefore often in kindly personal relations with their employer, the farmer, at whose board the unmarried hands took their meals, cooked by the farmer's wife.

(TREVELYAN—*English Social History*.)

EXERCISES

A. One of the following passages is quoted exactly from an exciting short story. In the other, after the first sentence, the ratio of word-clusters to sentences has been altered. Which of the two versions is the original? Why?

Version (1)	*Version (2)*
Lying thus, I held my breath till the very beatings of my heart seemed to suffocate me, and the veins in my temples were almost bursting. As I could bear it no longer, I rose to the surface,	Lying thus, I held my breath till the very beatings of my heart seemed to suffocate me, and the veins in my temples were almost bursting. I could bear it no longer. I rose to the surface. I

Version (1)	*Version (2)*
where I breathed again. I looked and listened, but all was darkness and silence, as my pursuers were gone by.	breathed again. I looked. I listened. All was darkness and silence. My pursuers were gone by.

B. In Edgar Allan Poe's short story *The Pit and the Pendulum* the writer is supposedly captured by the Inquisition and tied to a bench beneath a razor-sharp blade which swings like a pendulum above him, gradually approaching nearer every moment. I have spoilt the account of the approaching climax by joining together many of the short sentences. Rewrite the passage in effective short sentences and then compare your version with the original, which contains seven sentences:—

Down—certainly, relentlessly down, until it vibrated within three inches of my bosom, while I struggled violently—furiously—to free my left arm, which was free only from the elbow to the hand, which I could reach, from the platter beside me, to my mouth, with great effort, but no farther. Could I have broken the fastenings above the elbow, I would have seized and attempted to arrest the pendulum, but I might as well have attempted to arrest an avalanche!

CHAPTER XXV

KIND OF WORD-CLUSTERS

The four passages we have examined vary considerably in style. This variety arises partly from the different proportions of Clauses, Main and Subordinate, they contain:—

> Passage A (Old Joe) relies almost entirely on Simple Sentences.
> Passage B (Dr. Johnson) uses the Compound-Complex Sentence.
> Passage C (Mr. Churchill) contains a mixture, mainly of Simple and Compound Sentences.
> Passage D (Trevelyan) consists of two Complex Sentences.

Here again, as with the number of Word-Clusters, two opposing claims are at work:—

Interest demands Variety
but
Emphasis demands Repetition

The possibilities of VARIETY in kinds of word-cluster are enormous. The changes may be rung on:—

> Simple Sentences without Phrases.
> Simple Sentences with a varying number of Phrases.
> Compound, Complex and Compound-Complex Sentences with varying numbers and types of clauses, and with or without phrases of various kinds.

KIND OF WORD-CLUSTERS

Here is a passage—by no means exceptional—making good use of this variety:—

Passage E

I love to think of those Norwegian men who set out eagerly before the north-east wind when it came down from their mountains in the month of March like a god of great stature to impel them to the West. They pushed their long keels out upon the rollers, grinding the shingle of the beach at the fjord-head. They ran down the calm narrows, they breasted and they met the open sea. Then for days and days they drove under this monster of theirs and high friend, having the wind for a sort of captain, and looking always out to the sea line to find what they could find. It was the spring-time, and men feel the spring upon the sea even more surely than they feel it upon the land.

(HILAIRE BELLOC—*On a Great Wind.*)

This passage can be analysed roughly as follows:—

	Type of Cluster	*Type of Sentence*
I love to think of those Norwegian men	Main Clause	
who set out eagerly before the north-east wind	Adj. Clause	
when it came	Adv. Cl. Time	Complex
down from their mountains in the month of March like a god of great stature to impel them to West.	Adv. Phrases of Place, Time, Comparison, Reason	

134   PATTERN IN ENGLISH

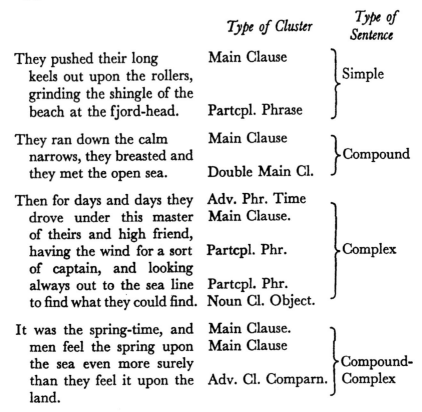

EXERCISE

Analyse the following passage on the same lines as Passage E above:—

When he spoke every one instantly understood how this voice had stopped a train. He was a dull-looking man with flat black hair, a colourless face, and a faint suggestion of the East in the level slits in his eyes and mouth. His blood and name, indeed, had remained dubious, ever since Sir Aaron had 'rescued' him from a waitership in a London restaurant, and (as some said) from more infamous things. But his voice was as vivid as his face was dead. Whether through exactitude in a foreign language, or in deference to his master (who had been somewhat deaf), Magnus's tones had a peculiarly ringing and piercing quality, and the whole group quite jumped when he spoke.

(G. K. CHESTERTON—*Three Tools of Death.*)

* * *

As we have already seen (page 126), it is sometimes well for Variety to yield, in the interests of emphasis, to REPETITION. Various special effects can be obtained by repetition of the various types of Sentence.

1. REPETITION of the SIMPLE SENTENCE was used effectively in the 'Old Joe' extract. Here is another example, from Edgar Allan Poe's story, *The Pit and the Pendulum.* Why does the writer use so many Simple Sentences? Is it effective?

PASSAGE F

Nor had I erred in my calculations—nor had I endured in vain. I at length felt that I was free. The surcingle hung in ribbons from my body. But the stroke of the pendulum already pressed upon my bosom. It had divided the serge of the robe. It had cut through the linen beneath. Twice again it swung, and a sharp sense of pain shot through every nerve. But the moment of escape had arrived. At a wave of my hand my deliverers (i.e. rats) hurried tumultuously away. With a steady movement—cautious, sidelong, shrinking, and slow—I slid from the embrace of the bandage, and beyond the reach of the scimitar. For the moment, at least, I was *free.*

2. REPETITION of the COMPOUND SENTENCE can be effective when used to pile up a series of statements all

contributing to one large-scale impression. The English Bible makes constant and successful use of this device:—

Passage G

And the Philistines fought, and Israel was smitten, and they fled every man into his tent: and there was a very great slaughter; for there fell of Israel 30,000 footmen. And the ark of God was taken; and the two sons of Eli, Hophni and Phinehas, were slain. (1 Samuel.)

The danger in using series of Compound Sentences—and, for that matter, Simple Sentences too—is that you may compile merely a list or catalogue, with no cumulative effect. Joseph Conrad, who makes considerable use of Simple and Compound Sentences, is skilful at avoiding this danger:—

Passage H

And we pumped. And there was no break in the weather. The sea was white like a sheet of foam, like a cauldron of boiling milk; there was not a break in the clouds, no—not the size of a man's hand—no, not for so much as ten seconds. There was for us no sky, there were for us no stars, no sun, no universe—nothing but angry clouds and an infuriated sea. (From *Youth*.)

EXERCISES

A. The danger of ineffective repetition of Compound Sentences is not avoided in this passage from a schoolboy essay. Rewrite it effectively:—

The cinema seemed to be stuffy, and I thought it was because there were so many people in there, but that was not the real reason. A fire had broken out in the projection-room and the operator was unable to put it out. Smoke belched out into the hall and people screamed and hurried towards the exits but they could not get out. Panic seized them, so they fought to escape and some of them were trampled underfoot.

B. The following extract from Malory's *Morte D'Arthur* contains too many Compound Sentences to suit modern taste. Rewrite it suitably:—

And then he mounted upon his horse and rode into a forest, and held no highway. And as he looked afore him he saw a fair plain, and beside that a fair castle, and afore the castle were many pavilions of silk and of divers hues. And him seemed that he saw there five hundred knights riding on horseback, and there were two parties; they that were of the castle were all on black horses, and their trappings black. And they that were without were all on white horses and trappings: and every each hurtled to other, that it marvelled Sir Lancelot.

* * *

3. REPETITION of the COMPLEX SENTENCE. The Simple and Compound Sentence structures are often sufficient for passages of narrative and description. The writer selects the essentials and leaves out much of the rest. But ideas cannot be treated so simply. They need to be set in their patterns of circumstances; hence the need for 'if', 'when', 'which', 'that', and so on— that is, for the Complex Sentence.

George Bernard Shaw writes a clear, pithy prose which makes good use of the short Simple Sentence. Nevertheless his ideas can often be expressed adequately only in series of Complex Sentences:—

Passage J

When Abernethy, the famous doctor, was asked why he indulged himself with all the habits he warned his patients against as unhealthy, he replied that his business was that of a direction post, which points out the way to a place, but does not go thither itself. He might have added that neither does it compel the traveller to go thither, nor prevent him from seeking some other way. Unfortunately our clerical direction posts always do coerce the traveller when they have the political power to do so. When the Church was a temporal as well as a spiritual power, and for long after to the full extent to which it could control or influence the temporal power, it enforced conformity by persecutions that were all the more ruthless because their intention was so excellent. Today, when the doctor has succeeded to the priest, and can do practically what he likes with parliament and the press through the blind faith in him which has succeeded to the far more critical faith in the parson, legal compulsion to take the doctor's prescription, however poisonous, is carried to an extent that would have horrified the Inquisition and staggered Archbishop Laud.

(From Preface to *St. Joan.*)

CHAPTER XXVI

ORDER OF WORD-CLUSTERS

Without breaking the Rule of Proximity, which requires that things thought of together should be expressed together, there is often a choice in the order of items. In the simplest case items X and Y may be next to each other either as X-Y or as Y-X:—

Though he was unwell he attended the meeting.

OR

He attended the meeting, though he was unwell.

The first of these sentences, where the main Statement is held back till the end, is an example of the SUSPENDED (or PERIODIC) SENTENCE. The second, in which the main statement is made first and the remaining information follows, is a LOOSE SENTENCE.

In both cases the Main Clause ('he attended the meeting') receives the main emphasis; but in the first case the Subordinate Clause ('though he was unwell'), being at the beginning of the sentence, attracts more attention than when, as in the second case, it is added as a kind of afterthought.

Further examples are:—

SUSPENDED (PERIODIC)	LOOSE
Holding his rifle in front of him, he advanced warily.	He advanced warily, holding his rifle in front of him.
To everybody who protested he gave the same reply.	He gave the same reply to everybody who protested.

SUSPENDED (PERIODIC)	LOOSE
The result, which had seemed a foregone conclusion, surprised us all.	We were all surprised at the result, which had seemed a foregone conclusion.

The difference in effect of these two types of construction is a matter of emphasis. In the Suspended Sentence one climbs up, as it were, to the climax. In the Loose Sentence one starts at the peak and descends.

There is a third construction—the BALANCED SENTENCE—in which the emphasis is shared equally by two or more items:—

I came; I saw; I conquered.

In practice there are variations and combinations of the three sentence-structures. For example:—

(a) Though he preferred tennis to cricket and never turned up to net practice, he often kept wicket for the first eleven, when there was no other wicket-keeper available.

(Suspended into Loose.)

(b) He suddenly stopped, when he saw the body on the floor, and, with a look of horror, sank into a nearby chair.

(Loose into Suspended.)

The opposing principles of Variety and Repetition can again be detected. Variety suggests that the Main Predications should not always be in the same position. Repetition urges that sometimes extra emphasis can be gained by a series of units in which the Main Predication comes repeatedly first or repeatedly last.

Suspended, Loose and Balanced rhythms are all present in the following passage:—

Passage K

When I saw her first there was a smoke of mist about her as high as her foreyard (*Suspended*). Her topsails and flying kites had a faint glow upon them where the dawn caught them (*Loose*). Then the mist rolled away from her, so that we could see her hull and the glimmer of the red sidelight as it was hoisted inboard (*Loose*). She was rolling slightly, tracing an arc against the heaven, and as I watched her the glow upon her deepened, till every sail she wore burned rosily like an opal turned to the sun, like a fiery jewel (*Loose, into Suspended, into Loose*). She was radiant, she was of an immortal beauty, that swaying, delicate clipper (*Balanced*). Coming as she came out of the mist into the dawn, she was like a spirit, like an intellectual presence (*Suspended*).

(MASEFIELD—*A Tarpaulin Muster.*)

Examples of Repetition of the three primary Sentence rhythms are:—

Passage L—Repetition of the Suspended Sentence

By transferring his army across the Shenandoah, and burning the bridge at Port Republic, Jackson could easily have escaped Fremont, and have met Shields in the Luray Valley with superior force. But the plain where the battle must be fought was commanded by the bluffs on the left bank of the Shenandoah; and should Fremont advance while an engagement was in progress, even though he could not cross the stream, he might assail the Confederates in flank with his numerous batteries. In order, then, to gain time in which to deal with

Shields, it was essential that Fremont should be held back, and this could only be done on the left bank. Further, if Fremont could be held back until Shields' force was annihilated, the former would be isolated. If Jackson could hold the bridge at Port Republic, and also prevent Fremont reaching the bluffs, he could recross when he had done with Shields, and fight Fremont without fear of interruption.   (Lt.-Col. HENDERSON—*Stonewall Jackson*.)

PASSAGE M—REPETITION OF THE LOOSE SENTENCE

She began singing very low, till his fingers dropped from hers, and his head sank on his breast. Then I told her to hush, and not stir, for fear she should wake him. We all kept as mute as mice a full half-hour, and should have done so longer, only Joseph, having finished his chapter, got up and said that he must rouse the master for prayers and bed. He stepped forward, and called him by name, and touched his shoulder, but he would not move, so he took the candle and looked at him. I thought there was something wrong as he set down the light, and seizing the children each by an arm, whispered to them to 'frame upstairs, and make little din; they might pray alone that evening—he had sommat to do.'   (EMILY BRONTE—*Wuthering Heights*.)

PASSAGE N—REPETITION OF THE BALANCED SENTENCE

Reading maketh a full man; conference a ready man; and writing an exact man. And therefore, if a man write little, he had need have a great memory;

if he confer little, he need have a present wit; and if he read little, he need have much cunning, to seem to know that he doth not. Histories make men wise; poets witty; the mathematics subtle; natural philosophy deep; moral grave; logic and rhetoric able to contend. (BACON—*Of Studies.*)

EXERCISES

A. Classify the following sentences as Suspended, Loose or Balanced:—

 (i) The regatta was cancelled because a gale was blowing.
 (ii) Those who like symphonies and classical music listen mainly to the Home Service; those who prefer light music and variety listen to the Light Programme.
 (iii) Provided you look after it and let me have it back by Tuesday, you may borrow my camera.
 (iv) Horses sweat; men perspire; women tingle.
 (v) He promised to sell a hundred tickets, though he knew very few people and had little time to spare.

B. Join these statements together to make Sentences of the kind indicated, making such alterations of phrasing as become necessary:—

 (i) The typist saw the flames.
  She immediately telephoned for the fire brigade.
   (Suspended.)
 (ii) He held the tyre under water.
  He later found the puncture.
   (Loose.)

(iii) The sonatas were more brilliant.
He composed them as a youth.
The fugues were more profound.
He wrote them as a man of experience.
(Balanced.)

(iv) The disease is detected at an early stage.
The patient is isolated.
Leprosy can be cured.
(Suspended.)

(v) He realised his danger.
He had practically no food.
He was miles from the nearest civilisation.
He could not move the boulder which blocked the way.
(Loose.)

C. What is noteworthy about the sentence structure of:—

I confess, it was want of consideration that made me an author. I writ, because it amused me. I corrected, because it was as pleasant to me to correct as to write. I published, because, I was told, I might please such as it was a credit to please.

(ALEXANDER POPE.)

PART SIX

APPENDICES

CHAPTER XXVII

APPENDIX A: PREPOSITIONS, ADVERBS AND CONJUNCTIONS

The fact that certain words may be used as any of these three Parts of Speech sometimes causes difficulty.

What Part of Speech is 'after' in each of the following sentences?

(1) Soon *after* Macbeth became king, he had Banquo murdered.
(2) Soon *after* that, Macduff fled to England.
(3) Soon *after*, Macbeth again visited the Witches.

There is no magic value in the names of the Parts of Speech themselves, but they help to remind you of the different jobs they do:—

In (1) the Conjunction 'after' introduces a Subordinate Adverb Clause of Time.
In (2) the Preposition 'after' governs the Pronoun 'that', making with it an Adverb Phrase of Time.
In (3) the Adverb of Time 'after' extends 'visited'.

Sentence (3) is unsatisfactory, because only the comma saves it from reading:—

Soon after Macbeth again visited the Witches.

This starts like (1) with an Adverb Clause, but the full-stop after 'Witches' forces one to re-read it like (3), with a simple Adverb. The difficulty can be avoided by using the more distinctive Adverb 'afterwards':—

Soon *afterwards*, Macbeth again visited the Witches.

EXERCISES

A. Write groups of three sentences, using the following words as Prepositions, Adverbs and Conjunctions:—

before, since, but

B. What Part of Speech is the italic word in each of the following:—

 (i) I stepped *off* the train.
 (ii) The bus stopped and I stepped *off*.
 (iii) Her friend did not wait *for* her.
 (iv) She hated the office, *for* it gave her a headache.
 (v) *When* crossing the road, look both ways.
 (vi) *When* you can, use a Belisha crossing.
 (vii) Public-houses are often *near* churches.
 (viii) There were no shops *near*.
 (ix) *As* this is a first offence, I shall overlook it.
 (x) Never disguise yourself *as* a policeman.

C. As she walked *down* the street, she noticed that the shutters of all the shops were *down*.

Here the first 'down' is a Preposition, the second an Adverb. Write sentences using each of the following words similarly:—

in, inside, beyond, through, over, beneath, on—and any other suitable words of this kind.

D. Prepositions and Adverbs are useful little words, but they should not be used in excess, as they are in the following sentences. Rewrite the sentences in improved style:—

(i) Bottom returned with an ass's head on.
(ii) At the station we met up with some friends.
(iii) Never jump off of a moving tramcar.
(iv) He was not hurt sufficiently enough to go to hospital.
(v) He climbed up over the wall.

CHAPTER XXVIII

APPENDIX B: ADVERBS AND ADJECTIVES

Adverbs and Adjectives are very closely connected. The same word may sometimes be used as either:—

He arrived *late*. (Adverb extending Verb 'arrived'.)
He was too *late*. (Adjective Complement of 'he'.)

Similarly, the same Preposition-Phrase may be used either Adjectively or Adverbially:—

The man *with the gun* was a lunatic.
   (Adjective Phrase extending 'man'.)
He threatened them *with the gun*.
   (Adverb Phrase extending Verb 'threatened'.)

This similarity makes it all the more important to distinguish between the two functions. One should write:—

> Please do not talk so *loudly*.
> (Not: Please do not talk so *loud*.)

Notice, however, that the following are quite correct:

> The dinner smells *good*.
> She looks *pretty*.

These are not Adverbs, but Adjectival Subject-Complements.

EXERCISES

A. Explain and correct the faults in the following:—

   (i) Come quick!
   (ii) The rain came on heavier.
   (iii) Hold on tight.
   (iv) If you do the job good, I will treat you handsome.
   (v) The train was painfully slow; it could hardly have gone slower without stopping.

B. What Parts of Speech are the words in italics?

   (i) Press *hard*.
   (ii) A dead heat seemed *likely*.
   (iii) A dead heat is *probably* the fairest decision.
   (iv) The *livelier* the music, the *quieter* seemed the audience.
   (v) *Kindly* return the empty bottles.

C. Write pairs of sentences showing that the following words can be used either as Adjectives or as Adverbs:—

early	late	hard	well
kindly	little	much	still
better	daily		

CHAPTER XXIX

APPENDIX C: PREPOSITIONS

Prepositions, as their name implies (Latin *praepositus* = placed before), normally precede the Noun or Pronoun they govern. It used to be argued, in fact, that they should *always* precede, and that above all a Sentence (or for that matter, a Phrase) must never end with a Preposition.

Writers sometimes went to ridiculous lengths to avoid ending with a Preposition. For example:—

This is that for which I have been hoping.

instead of the neater:—

This is what I have been hoping for.

It is said that, when Mr. Churchill came across a clumsy sentence like the former of these, he commented in the margin:—

This is the sort of English up with which I will not put.

There can be no rule of thumb in matters like this. Common sense requires the clearest and neatest word order available.

It is mainly in connection with the Relative Pronoun (who, which, that, etc.) that the positioning of the Preposition can be a matter of choice. One must be careful, though, to choose one or other of the alternatives, and not to include both, as in:—

The aeroplane is used for purposes *of* which people never think *about*.

Certain words are—or should be—followed by certain Prepositions. For example:—

> different *from*
> opposite *to*
> unaware *of*
> to free *from*

EXERCISE

Explain and correct the faults in the following:—

(i) Here is the hotel at which we always stay in.
(ii) The boy for whom I had been waiting for did not arrive until much later.
(iii) I bought an old car which the previous owner had travelled thousands of miles in.
(iv) To which of these boys did you give it?
(v) In an antique shop I found exactly that for which I was looking.
(vi) The question-paper was very different to what he had expected.
(vii) There was very rarely any disagreement among the two families.
(viii) He was quite unconscious and indifferent to any criticism.
(ix) I prefer horse-riding than any other pastime.
(x) What did you take away the book I was writing my essay in for?

CHAPTER XXX

APPENDIX D: TENSE

A Verb, broadly speaking, denotes a happening. Its form varies in TENSE according to the time-relationship between the happening itself and the use of the Verb (in speech or writing) to denote the happening:—

Tense
PRESENT: The Cambridge boat *is* half a length ahead.
PAST: Oxford *won* the toss.
FUTURE: The two crews *will have* dinner together after the race.

In these three cases the time of the happening is respectively the same as, earlier than, and later than the time of commenting on it.

There is a fourth, less obvious Tense, clumsily but accurately described as the Future in the Past:—

FUTURE IN THE PAST: The Oxford coxswain realised that it *would be* a hard race.

Here the time of comment is later than the time of happening, and the tense is therefore Past. But there is a further relationship of time between the two Past Tense Verbs 'realised' and 'would be'. At the time of 'realising', the hardness of the race was still in the Future. The would/should form of the Verb is used to indicate this subsidiary relationship.

In addition to showing Time, the Tense of the

Verb may indicate whether the happening is, was, or will be complete. Each of the four Simple Tenses we have examined has a corresponding Continuous Tense for use when the happening is unfinished or progressive:—

PRESENT CONTINUOUS: The two boats *are approaching* Putney Bridge.
PAST CONTINUOUS: The crowds *were gathering* early this morning.
FUTURE CONTINUOUS: They *will be returning* to their homes throughout the day.
FUTURE IN THE PAST CONTINUOUS: It was wrongly announced that we *should be televising* the race.

A further set of four forms—the Perfect Tenses—denote that the happening is 'perfected' or complete:—

PRESENT PERFECT: Cambridge *has won* several years in succession.
PAST PERFECT: The weather *had changed* completely.
FUTURE PERFECT: The race *will have finished* by 1.30 p.m.
FUTURE PERFECT IN THE PAST: No one *would have expected* such a result.

Finally, there are four forms—the Perfect Continuous Tenses—to indicate the completion of a happening until then continuous:—

PRESENT PERFECT CONTINUOUS: The team *has been practising* up to the last minute.

PAST PERFECT CONTINUOUS: It *had been raining* until an hour before starting time.

FUTURE PERFECT CONTINUOUS: By mid-day we *shall have been waiting* three hours.

FUTURE PERFECT IN THE PAST CONTINUOUS: He calculated that by mid-day he *would have been waiting* three hours.

Notice the connection between the Continuous Tense and the Present Participle, and between the Perfect Tense and the Past Participle. It would probably be more accurate to use the terms Continuous and Perfect Participles.

Compare: They *will* be returning.
with: We *shall* have been waiting.
And: No one *would have* expected.
with: We *should* be televising.

The situation with the sh- and w- forms is confused and confusing. Two Verbs, one indicating mere futurity, the other indicating a wish or determination about the future, have become mixed, leaving the First Person Singular and Plural forms different from the rest:—

Future	*Wish or Determination*
I shall, should	I will, would
thou wilt, wouldst	thou shalt, shouldest
he will, would	he shall, should
we shall, should	we will, would
you will, would	you shall, should
they will, would	they shall, should

Key-forms to remember are:—

>Thou *shalt* not kill. (Commandment, i.e. Determination.)
>
>I *will*. (marriage ceremonies, i.e. Wish.)

Compare also:—

>I *shall* drown and no one *will* save me.
>(Statement about the Future.)
>I *will* drown and no one *shall* save me.
>(Determination of a suicide.)

Any passage of speech or writing normally has a basic Tense. The first Finite Verb establishes that Tense, and the Tenses of the remaining Verbs are decided by their time-relationship to that first Verb.

The basic Tense, as we have already seen, is usually decided by the relationship between the time of comment and the time of the happening denoted: Past Tense for earlier events, Future Tense for later events, and so on.

One common exception to this procedure occurs when dealing with literature and the other arts. A work of art is as alive today as when it was created, and hence may be discussed in the Present Tense:—

>Falstaff *is* a fat knight who *figures* in several of Shakespeare's plays.

Notice that the Tense of 'is' determines the Tense of 'figures'.

Common sense is the best guide to the proper Sequence of Tenses, as it is called, but a few observations may help.

The Present Tense is used to denote an habitual or universal happening, even after a Past Tense:—

> I declined the invitation, as I *go* fishing on Saturdays.
> Galileo believed that the earth *goes* round the sun.

Sometimes we use the Present Tense when the Future would be more accurate:—

> I *leave* for Paris tomorrow.

In the hands of a skilled writer the occasional use of the Historic Present Tense—that is, describing past events in the Present Tense—can be very effective.

Dickens's *Tale of Two Cities* is a historical novel, and as such is written almost entirely in the Past Tense. But, at the end, to bring the tragic events closer to his readers and to suggest the timelessness of Sydney Carton's heroism, Dickens alternates between Past and Present Tenses, leaving the final emphasis on the Present.

Carton has taken the place—in the condemned cell of a Paris prison—of Charles Darnay, whom he closely resembles and for whom he is determined to die. While Carton, together with a little seamstress, goes to the guillotine, Darnay escapes to England:—

> As the patient eyes (of the little seamstress) were lifted to his (Carton's) face, he saw a sudden doubt in them, and then astonishment. He pressed the work-worn, hunger-worn young fingers, and touched his lips.
> 'Are you dying for him?' she whispered.
> 'And his wife and child. Hush! Yes.'
> 'O you will let me hold your brave hand, stranger?'
> 'Hush! Yes, my poor sister, to the last.'

The same shadows that are falling on the prison, are falling, in that same hour of the early afternoon, on the Barrier with the crowd about it, when a coach going out of Paris drives up to be examined.

* * *

'If she (Miss Pross) don't hear the roll of those dreadful carts, now very nigh their journey's end', said Mr. Cruncher, glancing over his shoulder, 'it's my opinion that indeed she never will hear anything else in this world.'

And indeed she never did.

Along the Paris streets, the death-carts rumble, hollow and harsh. Six tumbrils carry the day's wine to La Guillotine.

EXERCISES

A. Correct the Verbs in italics so that the Tenses shall be consistent:—

(i) They stab Caesar and his body *was taken* to the market-place.
(ii) I saw a curious object. Next day, I learnt that the object I *saw* was a mine.
(iii) Ben Gunn *was marooned* on Treasure Island three years before he was found by Jim Hawkins.
(iv) He later learnt that Frank had not been so lucky, but *was captured* by the Spaniards.
(v) When they finally traced her to a large island, they *meet* their cousin Eustace.
(vi) They carried telescopes in order to see of what nationality the ships *are*.

(vii) Gulliver was a sailor who *is* famous for his travels.
(viii) When not in use, the telescope can be shortened so that it *would not be* in the way.
(ix) They slay Cinna the poet merely because he *bore* the same name as one of the conspirators.
(x) Gulliver slept very soundly because the Lilliputians *drugged* the wine they *gave* him.

B. Fill in the correct sh . . . or w . . . form in the following:—

(i) All being well, we . . . go to the circus tomorrow.
(ii) The curfew . . . not ring tonight.
(iii) . . . you step this way, please?
(iv) If conditions continue favourable, several records . . . be broken today.
(v) He promised that he . . . be back in time.

C. Comment on the Tense of the Verbs in:—

(i) The football season begins next week.
(ii) Nero fiddled while Rome was burning.
(iii) You spend your money on ice-cream; I am saving up for a bicycle.
(iv) I saw that he was tired, but I did not know that he had been out all night.
(v) The Marathon runner realised that by midday he would have been running nine hours.

CHAPTER XXXI

APPENDIX E: STENCIL ANALYSIS

If the method of Simple Sentence analysis used in Part I is followed, it may be found helpful and time-saving to make a stencil of stiff paper or cardboard on the lines of the diagram below (page 160).

As soon as the notions of Subject and Predicate, Basis and Extension are established, these headings can be filled in and the three sets of rectangles cut out. This skeleton stencil can from then on be used for drawing 'boxes'.

As the various patterns are worked out, the detailed labels of the rectangles can be added. To make this easier, cross-references are given between the rectangles in the diagram below and the relevant pages of the text. The first four 'boxes' of Stencil A, for instance, can be labelled when Chapter II has been studied—i.e. when page 24 has been reached.

The finished stencils, when 'framing' the analysed items, afford a quick and searching test of accuracy by raising suitable questions. Has the appropriate stencil been selected? Does the top line read like a fair skeleton summary of the sentence? Does each item 'framed' fit, in nature and function, the labels round it?

It is advisable at first for the teacher to select Simple Sentences which conform readily with the patterns, but, as the pupil becomes competent in analysis, border-line cases and then exceptions should be introduced, the strictness of application of the stencil being gradually relaxed until the method can eventually be abandoned.

PATTERN IN ENGLISH

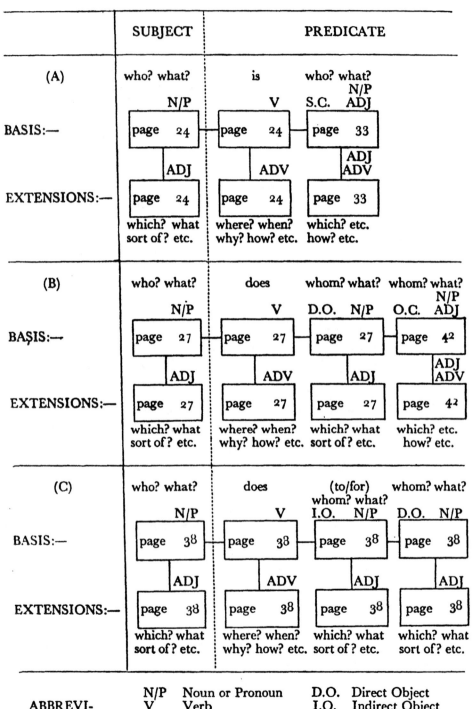

INDEX

ADJECTIVES, 23-24
    and Adverbs, Chap. XXVIII
    as Noun-Equivalents, 67
Adverbs, 23
    and Adjectives, Chap. XXVIII
    and Prepositions and Conjunctions, Chap. XXVII
    Relative, 96-97
Analysis, Clause, Part IV
Analysis, Subject/Predicate, Parts I-III
Antecedent, 105, 108
Apposition, 64, 75, 116-117

CASE, Chap. VIII
    Nominative, 50
    Objective, 50
    Possessive, 50-51
Clauses, 56, Part IV
    Adjective, 77, Chap. XVIII
        Restrictive, 107-108
    Adverb, 83, Chap. XIX
    Main, 100, 102
    Noun, 64, 67-68, Chap. XX
Commands, 15, 46-47
Complement:
    Noun-Clause as, 116
    Object-Complement, Chap. VI, 60
    Subject-Complement, Chap. IV, 148
Conjunctions:
    and Adverbs and Prepositions, Chap. XXVII
    Co-ordinating, 96, 101
    Subordinating, 96-98, 111, Chap. XXVII
Co-ordination, 95-96, 101-102

ELLIPSIS, 15-16, 47
Emphasis, 45, 135, 139-143

Equivalents, Part II
    Adjective-Equivalents, Chap. XII
    Adverb-Equivalents, Chap. XIII
    Noun-Equivalents, Chap. XI
    Verb-Equivalents, Chap. X
Exclamations, 48-49
Extensions, 23 *et seq.*

GERUND, 65-66

INTERJECTIONS, 49
'it', 64
'lay' and 'lie', 29

LINK-WORDS, Chap. XVI, 100, 105, 110-111, 115
    Continuative, 97
    Co-ordinating, 95-97
    Subordinating, 95-98

NOUNS, 16
    as Adjective-Equivalents, 74-75
    Number, 19, 62

OBJECT:
    Cognate, 30
    Direct, Chap. III, 66
    Indirect, Chap. V, 81-82
    Infinitive as, 66
    Noun Clause as, 116
    Provisional, 64
'only', 91-92

PARTICIPLES, 69-70, 154
    Past, 20-21, 69
    Present, 20, 67, 69
    Unrelated, 93

Person, 63
Phrases, 55
  Adjective, 69
  Noun, 116
  Participial, 69–70, 93
  Preposition, 71–73, 75, 80–82, 97–98, 115, 148
    'by'-Phrase, 82
    'to/for'-Phrase, 37–38, 81–82
Predicate, Chap. I
Prepositions, 72, 95, 96, 97, Chap. XXIX
  and Adverbs and Conjunctions, Chap. XXVII
  governing Noun Clauses, 116
  omission of, 73, 81
Pronouns, 16
  as Noun-Equivalents, 62-64
  Possessive, 50
  Relative, 96–97, 105–106, 108, 150
Proximity, Chap. XV, 108, 139

QUESTIONS, 47–48

SENTENCES:
  Complex, 95, 105 *et seq.*
    Repetition of, 137–138
  Compound, 95, Chap. XVII
    Repetition of, 135–136
  Compound-Complex, Chap. XXI, 128
  Length of, Chap. XXIV
  Simple, Part I, Chap. XIV, 129
    Repetition of, 135
  Suspended, Loose, Balanced, Chap. XXVI

'shall/will, should/would', 154–155
Stencil analysis, 24, 27, 33, 38, 42, Chap. XXXI
Subject, Chap. I
  Noun Clause as, 115–116
  Provisional, 64–65
Subordination, 95–97

TENSE, Chap. XXX
  Historic Present, 156–157
  Sequence of, 155–156
'there', 65

VERBS, 17 *et seq.*
  Active and Passive, 29, 37, 43, 70, 82
  Auxiliary, 20, 21
  Compound, 58–59
  Finite, 20
  of Incomplete Predication, 32, 41–42
  Infinitive, 21, 65–66
    as Adjective-Equivalent, 76
    as Adverb-Equivalent, 79
  Reflexive, 27
  Tense, Chap. XXX
  Transitive and Intransitive, 26, 28–30
Verb-Adjectives, 67
Verb-Nouns, 65–66
Voice, 29, 37, 43, 70, 82

'WILL/shall, would/should', 154–155
Word-Order, 12, 38, Chap. VII